What Life Was Like®

WHEN LONGSHIPS SAILED

Vikings
AD 800 ~ 1100

What Life Was Like

WHEN LONGSHIPS SAILED

Vikings
AD 800 ~ 1100

BY THE EDITORS OF TIME-LIFE BOOKS, ALEXANDRIA, VIRGINIA

CONTENTS

WHEN LONGSHIPS
SAILED

THE VENTURESOME VIKINGS

"Like men they traveled far for gold," proclaimed a memorial stone honoring a band of Swedes who died in battle while seeking fortune in a distant land. Such restlessness and daring were characteristic of the Vikings—the name applied today to all Scandinavians, at home or abroad, who lived during the expansive era of raiding, trading, and colonization that dawned around AD 800. That era began with devastating attacks by Norsemen against monasteries and other vulnerable targets along the coasts of England and the Continent, and the Vikings were portrayed ever after as bloody marauders. But they were settlers as well as invaders, explorers as well as plunderers, merchants as well as conquerors, creators as well as destroyers.

Long before they took the world by force, the Scandinavians were energetic traders. As early as 1500 BC, they were exchanging goods across the North Sea with the peoples of Ireland and England. By the first century AD, they were trading with the Romans, and by the fifth century, they were hosting foreign merchants at bustling Scandinavian market towns. Trade exposed them to the wealth of others and fed dreams of plunder and conquest.

To realize those dreams, the Scandinavians first had to master the art of shipbuilding. They had long crafted boats without sails in which they traversed their native fjords and even crossed the seas in good weather. But by the eighth century, they had evolved a formidable sailing vessel, the longship—fast, nimble, seaworthy, and capable of being beached along coasts or rowed far up rivers. The longship opened the world to the Vikings, and thousands of them seized the opportunity, driven by a hunger for land, adventure, or plunder.

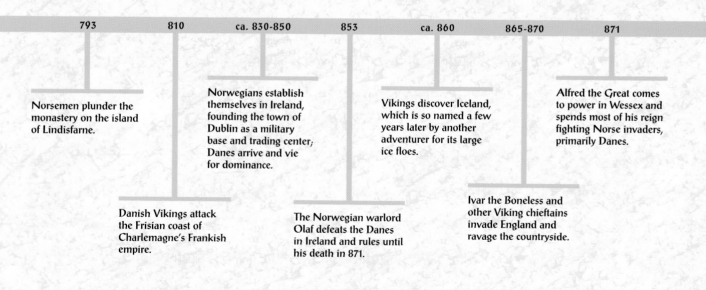

793

Norsemen plunder the monastery on the island of Lindisfarne.

810

Danish Vikings attack the Frisian coast of Charlemagne's Frankish empire.

ca. 830-850

Norwegians establish themselves in Ireland, founding the town of Dublin as a military base and trading center; Danes arrive and vie for dominance.

853

The Norwegian warlord Olaf defeats the Danes in Ireland and rules until his death in 871.

ca. 860

Vikings discover Iceland, which is so named a few years later by another adventurer for its large ice floes.

865-870

Ivar the Boneless and other Viking chieftains invade England and ravage the countryside.

871

Alfred the Great comes to power in Wessex and spends most of his reign fighting Norse invaders, primarily Danes.

On a June day in AD 793, Norsemen in longships descended on the island of Lindisfarne off the east coast of England and pillaged its treasure-laden monastery, killing many of the monks there and enslaving others. The assault shocked Christian Europe and marked the beginning of the violent Viking age. At first, the raids were limited to coastal areas and carried out by small bands, who retreated quickly with their booty. But before long, well-organized war parties from the emerging nations of Denmark, Sweden, and Norway, led by ambitious chieftains and kings, were invading foreign lands, exacting tribute, and seizing territory. In 810 the Danish king Godfred attacked the coast of Frisia (the Netherlands), then part of Charlemagne's empire. Buoyed by his initial success, Godfred talked of conquering Germany, but he died before he could carry out his plans, and Charlemagne

strengthened his defenses against future Viking threats.

The British Isles, divided into many rival kingdoms, were more vulnerable. During the course of the ninth century, Norwegian Vikings gained control of large parts of Ireland and founded Dublin, among other towns. Danish warriors vied with the Norwegians in Ireland for a while but made their greatest gains in England, claiming much of the country before King Alfred the Great, of Wessex, drove them out of southern England and relegated them to a large area in the north and east known as the Danelaw. Tens of thousands of Danes then turned their hostile attentions to France, venturing up the Seine River and laying siege to Paris in 885. Those invaders ultimately retreated, but Vikings became so well established along the coast that the French king later ceded to their chieftain, Rollo, the area known as Nor-

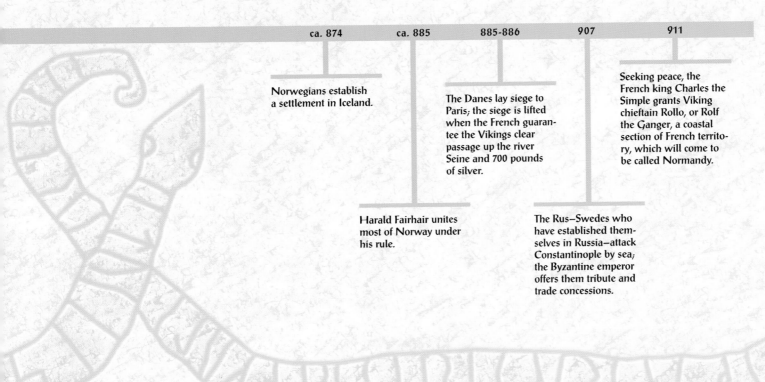

ca. 874

Norwegians establish a settlement in Iceland.

Harald Fairhair unites most of Norway under his rule.

ca. 885

The Danes lay siege to Paris; the siege is lifted when the French guarantee the Vikings clear passage up the river Seine and 700 pounds of silver.

885-886

907

The Rus–Swedes who have established themselves in Russia—attack Constantinople by sea; the Byzantine emperor offers them tribute and trade concessions.

911

Seeking peace, the French king Charles the Simple grants Viking chieftain Rollo, or Rolf the Ganger, a coastal section of French territory, which will come to be called Normandy.

mandy, named for the occupying Norsemen. Armed Swedes, meanwhile, were delving deep into Russia to collar slaves and trade with merchants from the Byzantine and Arab worlds at places such as Bulgar and Kiev, which became a Swedish stronghold. In time, Vikings reached all the way to the Mediterranean and the shores of North Africa.

Part of the impetus for this remarkable expansion came from unrest in the Scandinavian homeland, where assertive rulers such as Harald Fairhair of Norway were uniting their kingdoms at sword-point and displacing rival chieftains, some of whom then ventured abroad with their followers. The rise of Harald Fairhair was one of several factors that impelled thousands of Scandinavians—most of them Norwegians—to cross the North Atlantic and settle Iceland between 870 and 930. But the Vikings did not stop there. In 982 Icelander Erik the Red ventured westward and explored

Greenland, where he founded a colony a few years afterward. Carrying on in the tradition of his father, Erik, Leif Eriksson sailed off from Greenland into the unknown around the year 1000 and reached the shores of North America, charting the way for a short-lived Viking settlement at a place known as Vinland.

Back in Europe, meanwhile, the Viking age of conquest was building to a climax. By the 11th century, Christianity was supplanting the traditional Norse religion in Scandinavia, thanks to the determined efforts of Christian rulers like King Olaf Haraldsson (later known as Saint Olaf), who ascended the throne of Norway in 1015 and set about completing the conversion of his country by force. As his campaigns demonstrated, the advent of Christianity did nothing to pacify the region. Having consolidated their kingdoms, the monarchs of Scandinavia vied for supremacy with one

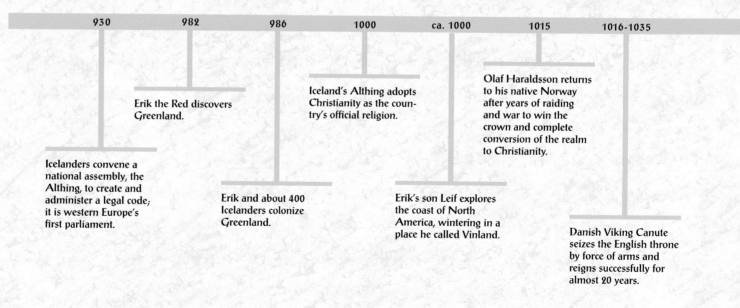

930   982   986   1000   ca. 1000   1015   1016-1035

Erik the Red discovers Greenland.

Iceland's Althing adopts Christianity as the country's official religion.

Olaf Haraldsson returns to his native Norway after years of raiding and war to win the crown and complete conversion of the realm to Christianity.

Icelanders convene a national assembly, the Althing, to create and administer a legal code; it is western Europe's first parliament.

Erik and about 400 Icelanders colonize Greenland.

Erik's son Leif explores the coast of North America, wintering in a place he called Vinland.

Danish Viking Canute seizes the English throne by force of arms and reigns successfully for almost 20 years.

another and with the rulers of England and Normandy. Among the most successful of those Viking warrior kings was Canute, who at one time ruled his native Denmark as well as Norway and England. The English throne subsequently reverted to local control, but England remained a bone of contention, coveted by outsiders who hoped to emulate Canute's feat. In 1066 a great struggle for control of England was played out between the English king Harold Godwinson, the Norwegian king Harald Hardradi, and William, duke of Normandy. The defeat of the Norwegians by the English—who then lost out to the Normans under William—signaled the end of the Viking era of expansion, for the victorious Normans had long since shed their Norse identity and embraced French ways.

Iceland and Greenland would remain lonely outposts of Viking culture until the 13th century, when they surrendered their independence and became possessions of Norway amid worsening weather conditions and other travails. Deeply attached to the old Norse traditions, the Icelanders set down in writing the sagas that elaborated artfully on their history and offered future generations a sweeping panorama of the Viking world—a place where stout-hearted women defended the interests of their households and sometimes drove their men to violent deeds, where lawspeakers and peacekeepers struggled heroically to resolve disputes and restore order, and where outlaws redeemed themselves by ranging abroad and claiming bountiful new lands for their followers. Those stories, together with the revealing works of Norse artisans that people carried with them to their graves, offer us a rich and rounded portrait of the Vikings— a people who owed their success as much to their adaptability and ingenuity as to their notorious ferocity.

1030	1066	ca. 1200	1261	1264

Norwegian king Harald Hardradi is killed by England's Harold Godwinson at the Battle of Stamford Bridge; Normandy's William the Conqueror then defeats Harold at the Battle of Hastings.

Greenlanders surrender their autonomy to Norway in return for trade concessions after their economy is disrupted by worsening weather conditions.

Internal dissension and economic problems bring an end to Iceland's independent government, and the king of Norway assumes control.

Olaf Haraldsson dies trying to regain his lost kingdom from Canute, who seized it in 1028; Olaf Haraldsson is subsequently canonized as Saint Olaf, patron saint of Norway.

Icelanders begin recording the Norwegian and Icelandic sagas transmitted orally since the 800s.

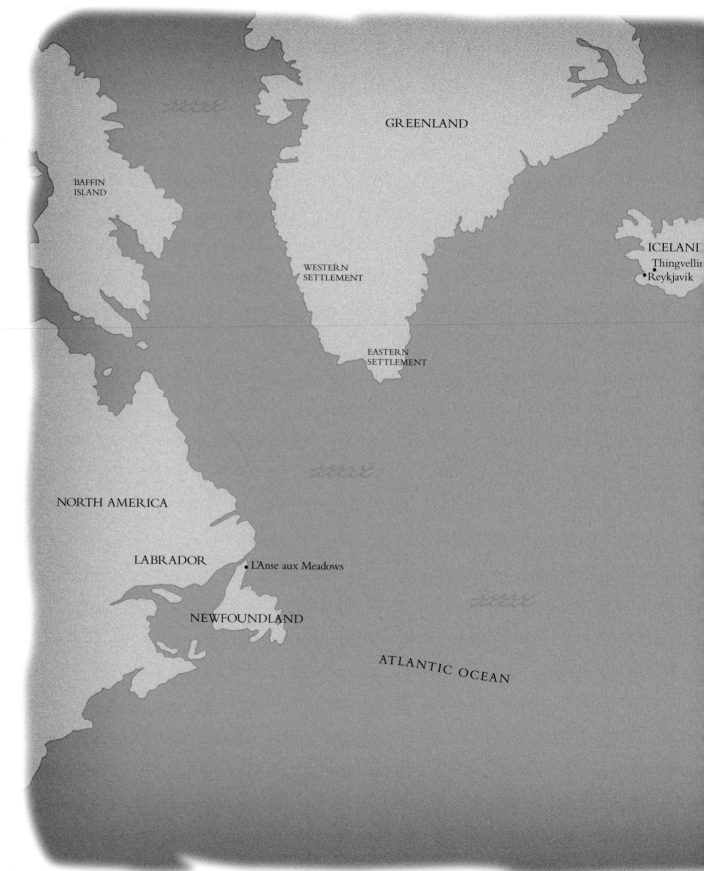

From AD 800 to 1100, Vikings left their homes in Scandinavia, the area comprising modern Norway, Sweden, and Denmark, traversed much of the known world, and ventured into the unknown. Some sailed east across the Baltic Sea, established trading bases at Staraya Ladoga and Novgorod, and journeyed down through Russia to Kiev and Bulgar, reaching as far as the Caspian Sea, where a few Norse traders left their boats behind and joined camel trains to Baghdad.

Others headed southwest and seized much of the British Isles, claimed Normandy, and delved into the Mediterranean. Great colonizers as well, Vikings peopled the Orkney, Shetland, and Faeroe Islands on their way to settling Iceland. Icelanders went on to establish two settlements in Greenland. Nearly 500 years before Columbus reached the New World, Norse colonists reached the shores of North America and lived briefly in Newfoundland.

GREENLAND

BAFFIN ISLAND

ICELAND

Thingvellir

Reykjavik

WESTERN SETTLEMENT

EASTERN SETTLEMENT

NORTH AMERICA

LABRADOR

L'Anse aux Meadows

NEWFOUNDLAND

ATLANTIC OCEAN

LAPLAND

HALOGALAND

NORWAY

FINLAND

FAEROE ISLANDS

Lake
Ladoga

•Staraya Ladoga

•Novgorod

TLAND ISLANDS

NEY ISLANDS

IDES

CAITHNESS

Stavanger•

VESTFOLD

SWEDEN

Birka•

•Helgö

Oseberg

GOTLAND

Kaupang

•Bulgar

RUSSIA

SCOTLAND

LINDISFARNE

Fyrkat•

NORTH SEA

DENMARK

BALTIC SEA

York•

•Stamford Bridge

Dublin•

DANELAW

•Hedeby

IRELAND

ENGLAND

London

WESSEX

•Hastings

FRISIA

Rhine River

ENGLISH CHANNEL

Bayeux•

NORMANDY

•Paris

Seine River

Dnieper River

Volga River

•Kiev

BLACK SEA

CASPIAN SEA

Constantinople•

BYZANTINE EMPIRE

SICILY

MEDITERRANEAN SEA

Baghdad•

13

CHAPTER ONE

STIRRINGS IN THE HOMELAND

Seated on his throne, King Harald Fairhair of Norway greets the Danish chieftain Guthrum in an illustration from an Icelandic manuscript chronicling the feats of great Vikings. While Guthrum campaigned abroad in the late ninth century and conquered part of England, Harald overpowered rivals at home and was celebrated as the first to rule "the whole of Norway."

oung Harald Fairhair of Norway had many a legend to live up to. Tales of his royal ancestors throbbed with power and magic. One fabled king among his forebears went chasing after a dwarf and disappeared into a boulder. Another cleared an entire forest with fire and ax before being sacrificed by his people to ensure the fertility of the land. Their queens were memorable as well. Harald's grandmother Asa was credited with sending a servant to murder her husband, Gudrod the Hunting King, by running him through with a spear. She had ample reason, for Gudrod had claimed her by killing her brother and her father (himself a king) and carrying her off like a common concubine. Restored to dignity by the bloodletting, Asa lived out her days in regal splendor. Perhaps it was she who was buried at Oseberg, by the shores of Oslo Fjord on Norway's southeast coast, in a mound containing a high-prowed ship laden with a wagon and sleighs, tapestries and household goods, and the bodies of a dozen or more horses, four dogs, and a slave woman—all put to death to accompany the great lady on her journey to the afterworld.

Harald learned further lessons in majesty from his father, Halvdan the Black. When Halvdan came to power, he was just one of many petty kings living in Norway. But his was perhaps the finest domain in the land—Vestfold, rising in lush green slopes along the western shores of Oslo Fjord and graced with splendid harbors and bustling markets. Profiting by that inheritance, Halvdan the Black spent his reign subduing the kings of neighboring territories and adding their domains to his own. When he died at the age of 40, it was said, his people insisted that the king's corpse be quartered, so that each of his provinces might have a part to bury and thus enrich their lands.

Harald was only 10 years old when he succeeded to this burgeoning kingdom in the latter half of the ninth century. His uncle, Guthorm, served as his regent for a while, but Harald soon asserted himself, for this was an age when a boy of 12 was on the verge of manhood and ready to go "a-viking," as Norsemen, or Scandinavians, referred to their exploits. According to one of his court skalds, or poets, Harald was "a lad in years but mature in all accomplishments that a courteous king ought to command. His hair grew thick, with a magnificent sheen very like fine silk. He was the most handsome of men, very strong and big of build."

Like other great Vikings, Harald surrounded himself with men of courage and cunning, and he supported them in grand style. In his long hall sat wise elders who advised him, fluent skalds who memorialized his deeds in verse, and sure-handed jugglers and jesters who amused the king and company by playing with fire or frolicking with a crop-eared dog. But none of his retainers gave Harald more pride and pleasure than the young fighting men drawn to him by his generosity. In the words of one skald:

> Well-rewarded are they, those famed in battle,
> Who sit gaming in Harald's hall. . . .
> By their clothing, their gold armlets
> You see they are the king's friends.
> They bear red cloaks, stained shields,
> Silver-clad swords, ringed mailcoats,
> Gilded sword belts, engraved helmets,
> Rings on their arms, as Harald gave them.

An imposing Viking woman with her hand on her hip restrains a man from attacking a rider and hound in this detail from a carved wagon buried at Oseberg with the remains of a lady of high rank. Viking women were portrayed as forceful figures, capable of averting bloodshed or provoking it.

No king responsible for such a keen and rapacious company of warriors could afford to keep them idle for long. From the early years of his reign, Harald was on the lookout for fresh lands to conquer and pillage. With Guthorm's assistance, he subdued several rival kings and enlarged his domain. But according to the Icelander Snorri Sturluson, who set down Harald's saga in writing several centuries later, the king harbored no ambition to master all of Norway until a spirited young woman put that task to him as a challenge.

When Harald was old enough to long for a woman in his bed, Snorri related, he sent his men after Gyda, daughter of King Erik of Hordaland, on Norway's rugged southwest coast. Kings sometimes entrusted their children's rearing to loyal followers, a practice called fosterage, and Gyda was being raised for Erik by a wealthy *bondi,* or landowner. Perhaps Harald assumed that a princess in such a setting could be taken lightly, for he wanted Gyda as his concubine. Like Harald's grandmother Asa, however, Gyda knew her worth and insisted on it. She informed Harald's men that she had no intention of wasting her maidenhood on one "who had not a bigger kingdom to rule than some shires." One day, Gyda added, she might consent to become Harald's proper wife, but only when "he had first for her sake laid under himself all Norway."

Harald's men relayed her defiant words to the king, fully expecting him to order Gyda "dishonored," or raped, in payment for her effrontery. Instead, the young king declared himself grateful to Gyda for reminding him of his duty. In true Viking fashion, he rose to her challenge. "Never shall my hair be cut or combed," he promised, "till I have possessed myself of all Norway."

Gyda was just one of many women in Viking lore who drove men to bold and merciless deeds. "Cold are women's counsels," ran a Norse proverb. And the people in Harald's path would no doubt have agreed. Unleashing his eager warriors, he rampaged northward, scorching villages as he went. To those who resisted, he offered the sword. To those who submitted and agreed to become his liegemen, however, he pledged peace and protection. Among the men who came to terms with Harald was a great chieftain of the north called Haakon Grjotgardson, who sealed his pact with the king by offering him his daughter in marriage. (Harald acquired several wives in such fashion even as he set about proving himself to Gyda.) With Haakon's help, Harald won control of the north, then mustered a fleet of longships, replete "with grim gaping heads and rich carved prows," and set out to secure the west coast, riven with fjords that offered shelter to his foes. In the end, only Gyda's father, King Erik, and his allies in the southwest remained defiant, and Harald crushed them in a great sea battle near Stavanger.

Having taken 10 grimy years to make good on his vow, Harald at last took a bath and combed his hair. A companion in arms cut it for him and gave him his famous epithet— Fairhair. As for the impertinent Gyda, she had little to celebrate. Her father had perished in battle, and by the time Harald took her in marriage, she had to share his favor with eight other wives. Eventually, he divorced Gyda along with the others, so that he could wed a Danish princess called Ragnhild the Mighty, who was apparently too grand to tolerate any domestic rivals.

A ROYAL SEND-OFF

Late one summer, mourners gathered along the shores of Oslo Fjord in southeast Norway to bury a Viking woman of high rank. The year was AD 834, as revealed by the rings of trees felled to build her burial chamber, and the site was the place known today as Oseberg, or Asa's Mound. Oseberg was within the ancient kingdom of Vestfold, where Harald Fairhair inherited power a few decades after the woman's death. Judging by the extravagant tribute paid to her, she was certainly one of the leading figures in Vestfold and may indeed have been Harald's grandmother, Queen Asa.

To transport the great lady to the next world, a splendid longship, measuring 71 feet from stem to stern, was brought ashore and lowered into a shallow pit. Attendants then laid the woman's body on a carved bed in a log burial chamber located behind the mast, amid walls adorned with a shimmering tapestry *(overleaf)*. So that the deceased would not make this journey alone, the attendants laid beside her the body of another woman, presumably her slave, sacrificed for the occasion.

The ship was lavishly equipped to sustain the lady and her companion, both in transit and at their destination. Among the gear were a full set of 30 oars, an intri-

Vikings load a dragon-headed long-ship for a journey to the afterworld in this rendering of a royal burial like the one at Oseberg.

A carved wagon from Oseberg shows the Viking flair for woodworking.

cately carved wagon, several sleighs, two tents, four more beds and a chair, wooden chests, brass-bound buckets—including one filled with wild apples—tools and seeds, looms, and kitchen utensils. Here as in other Viking ship burials, exotic items from abroad figured among the goods (one dead chieftain was honored with a peacock). At least a dozen horses were herded aboard the Oseberg ship and put to death.

When all was in place, the attendants cut down the mast so that it would not protrude from the barrow. Then they covered the ship and its occupants with a mound of stones, clay, and turf, thus preserving for posterity one of the great troves that Viking rulers sailed off with at death.

Majestic horses pull carts during a ceremonial procession in this reconstructed segment of the Oseberg tapestry, one of the few surviving examples of Viking needlework.

This ornate sleigh, one of four on the burial ship, was the kind used ceremonially when snow covered the ground.

Gyda's fabled challenge brought sorrow to herself and countless others, but it also provoked heroic deeds, and not only by Harald. His conquests displaced many proud men, and some then sailed off with their followers to lay claim to other settled lands or to plant colonies in desolate spots. "At that time great waste lands were peopled," Snorri wrote in reference to Viking migrations to the wind-swept Scottish isles, to the Faeroe Islands, and to his own beloved Iceland, settled by Norwegians around the time that Harald forged their homeland into one nation. Snorri traced his own ancestry to Vikings who had been ousted by Harald and did not cherish the king's memory. Yet he recognized that good as well as evil came of the fierce pride that impelled men like Harald to meet challenges and to prove themselves. Their fury was like a force of nature, at once destructive and creative. Driven by cold counsels and hot ambitions, they stirred up storms that engulfed the Viking homeland and swept across the seas, spelling ruin for some in their path and renewal for others.

Like all Norse sagas, Snorri's account of the rise of Harald Fairhair blended fact with fancy. Harald indeed fought his way to become king of Norway in the late ninth century, but parts of the country eluded his control, and his conquests were not the only factor encouraging Vikings to emigrate. By the time that Harald reached the height of his power, venturesome bands from the emerging nations of Norway, Denmark, and Sweden had been ranging abroad in force for roughly a century. Some of those fearsome raiders and colonists were ousted from Scandinavia by con-

querors like Harald, but others were simply pursuing opportunity overseas at a time when their prospects at home were severely constricted by a swelling population and when their sturdy ships and seawise ways made them the master mariners of the North Atlantic.

The Vikings who settled in populous places like England and Normandy intermingled with the local people and adopted their language and habits. In empty regions like Iceland, however, the Norse immigrants maintained a way of life much like the one they had known at home. Iceland became the great repository of Viking culture, preserving a vivid record of the customs and beliefs of the ancestral Norwegians—and by extension, the early Scandinavians as a whole, for the various Viking peoples shared a common language and heritage.

At home and abroad, the Vikings flourished in difficult circumstances because there was much more to their culture than just feuding and fighting. They were thrifty and industrious, and they knew how to make the most of limited resources, whether through farming, herding, or fishing. They had a keen instinct for trade as well. By Harald's time, the Vikings were fast becoming the shopkeepers of Europe. Trading centers such as Hedeby in Denmark, Birka in Sweden, and Kaupang in Harald's Vestfold were growing into rich and important towns, and kings were tapping the profits derived from that trade in order to support their own ambitions.

Vikings did not have to raid or conquer to achieve distinction, for trading sorties could be just as rewarding. One bold Norwegian merchant named Ottar, from the far northern province of Halogaland, found his way in the late ninth century to the court of King Alfred the Great in England and so impressed the monarch that Alfred devoted part of a book he was compiling to the story of this remarkable Viking.

Alfred's scribes did not record the circumstances that brought Ottar to their court. Most likely the merchant went there to trade, for he was evidently on good terms with the king, and that in itself was surprising. Since coming to power in AD 871,

The Viking craftsman who owned this oak tool chest, unearthed in Sweden, packed it with more than 200 items, including shears, tongs, saws, axes, files, and other tools used to work both wood and metal. The owner may have been a shipbuilder or a jack-of-all-trades.

Alfred had spent most of his reign fighting Norse invaders, primarily Danes, finally achieving a treaty with them by which he retained a corner of England, to the south and west, including his native kingdom of Wessex, below the Thames River. The territory to the north and east was known as the Danelaw, held by Viking settlers.

Reasonably secure, Alfred set out to rehabilitate a society that had been ravaged by a century of Viking marauding. He constructed fortified towns throughout his lands, and he salvaged what little remained of the monastery-based culture the Norsemen had pillaged. Part of his plan was the translation from Latin into Anglo-Saxon of a few books he thought "most needful for men to know," one of which was a history of the world written in the fifth century by a priest named Paulus Orosius. When Ottar arrived at Alfred's court bearing gifts of walrus ivory and seeking his protection, the king welcomed him—and made sure that the visitor's account of his little-known Viking world was included in the geographical survey that constituted part of the history.

Perhaps they sat in Alfred's stone hall at Winchester, with its frescoed walls, where Ottar told tales of his homeland that were dutifully recorded by the king's scribes, whose own language was fairly close to the Norse spoken by Ottar. No doubt the scribes were awed by this emissary from a strange and forbidding country, so unlike their green and gentle Wessex.

Ottar informed the king with a touch of pride that he lived "the furthest north of all Norwegians." His home district of Halogaland reached up into the Arctic, and its rocky coastline supported only a few Viking settlements. Farther inland lived members of a distinct group that Ottar called the Finnas, or Lapps, whose many occupations included herding reindeer; hunting in the colder

Undaunted by wintry landscapes like this one in Norway, the Vikings moved about on sleighs, skis, or skates *(inset)* carved from animal bone and fastened to leather shoes with a thong. Made for stability rather than for speed, such skates worked like short skis. Instead of gliding across the ice, skaters propelled themselves forward with iron-tipped poles.

months for elk, fox, marten, mink, and other furbearing creatures; and foraging in the summer along the coast, where they fished, gathered eggs and down from the nests of birds, and pursued whales, walruses, and seals.

Ottar owed much of his prosperity to the Lapps. He had a small farm in Halogaland, but the land there was not lush and the growing season was short, and he was considered to be poor in livestock according to English standards. "He was among the most important men of that country," Alfred's scribes noted, "but for all that he possessed no more than twenty cattle and twenty sheep and twenty pigs, and what little he ploughed, he ploughed with horses."

Ottar's real wealth came in the form of the tribute paid him by the Lapps, no doubt in exchange for the freedom to follow their traditional ways unmolested. "Each pays according to his rank," the chronicle recorded, with the highest in rank offering up "the skins of fifteen martens, five reindeer and one bear," along with a short coat of bear or otter skin, 10 bushels of down (culled most likely from the feathery nests of the eider ducks that flourished in the far north) and two ship's cables, one of whale hide and the other of seal hide, obtained by cutting the tough skin from those animals in a long spiral strip.

Part of the tribute Ottar and others collected from the Lapps may have been claimed by Harald Fairhair as his royal due, but Ottar made no mention of such an obligation. (Perhaps he felt it would be impolitic to refer to a rival king in Alfred's presence.) In any case, Ottar's share of the tribute left him plenty to offer in trade, and he increased his wealth by doing some herding and hunting of his own. He had an impressive herd of 600 tame reindeer, including six valuable decoys, which were used to lure wild reindeer into a position where they could be caught. Ottar not-

ed that the animals were still "unsold" when he left home, indicating that he kept them not for subsistence but in hopes of turning a profit.

Ottar and his fellow Vikings of the far north also emulated the Lapps by hunting walruses and whales. Walruses yielded splendid ivory from their tusks—Ottar could think of no finer item to offer Alfred when he arrived at the court—and their hide was even better than that of whales or seals for making rope or cable. The skin of a walrus, cut in a spiral from tail to head, made a rope nearly 10 times as long as the animal itself, and one strong enough to bind loads of tree trunks. As for whales, Ottar boasted that he and five companions once killed 60 of them in two days. The largest of those leviathans, he claimed, measured up to 50 ells long, or nearly 200 feet. That figure was either a gross exaggeration or an error in translation, since the Anglo-Saxons and the Vikings were still mastering each other's terms. Whatever the size of those whales, however, such a haul meant a bonanza of meat, bone, and blubber, which would be rendered into oil for lamps.

Plainly, Ottar was a man of many parts—and ports. He detailed to his English hosts his lengthy trading ventures as well as his various destinations. The merchant frequently sailed south from Halogaland with his wares, hugging the coast of Norway

Toys like this wooden horse and boat encouraged Viking children to be imaginative in their play. In place of formal schooling, youngsters mastered skills by helping their elders. Boys prepared for war by sparring with each other, and children of both sexes learned to be adaptable and outgoing by spending time with foster families.

until he rounded the tip and put in at Kaupang on Oslo Fjord. The journey to that Norwegian trading town could take him about a month, he pointed out, assuming that he had a favorable wind and put in to shore each night, as prudent Vikings generally did when they were close to land.

Ottar felt no obligation to unload his wares only at Kaupang, where the king's agents may well have been waiting to take their toll. He knew the way to Hedeby, just five days' journey south of Kaupang on the east coast of Denmark. The straits leading there were haunted by pirates, forcing traders to travel in convoys, but Ottar found the journey worth his while and no doubt felt at home at Hedeby. At a time when the various peoples of Scandinavia still spoke the same basic language and identified themselves more by their local districts than by nationality, he probably cared little whether a Norwegian king or a Danish one benefited by his trade. Indeed, his cordial relationship with Alfred suggested that he would be more than happy to include among his royal patrons

that celebrated foe of Norsemen. Adaptable and opportunistic, Ottar embodied the spirit that carried Vikings profitably to the far corners of the old world—and to new worlds beyond.

Although many Vikings embarked on journeys as ambitious as Ottar's, few were as free as he was to chart their own course. Scandinavians raised like Ottar in far northern areas or remote coastal spots may have felt fewer restraints than those in more populous areas, but Viking society as a whole had distinct classes and well-defined rules. Boys and girls came of age knowing where they stood in the community and what their obligations were. Law, tradition, and mythology defined their roles and responsibilities.

An old myth, preserved in the Icelandic poem *Rigsthula*, explained how the Vikings came to be divided up into classes. In this tale, the god Rig, or Heimdall, the father of humanity, wandered the world in search of refuge until he arrived at a sad little hut inhabited by an elderly couple named Ai and Edda, or Great-Grandfather and Great-Grandmother. Their clothes were old and worn, and all they could offer Rig to eat was a hunk of dark bread and some broth. Rig stayed with them three nights and slept between them in their bed, then went on his way.

Nine months later Great-Grandmother gave birth to a son called Thrall. He was a swarthy, clumsy creature, with a humpback and big feet, and he mated with a girl as ill-formed as he was and spawned a brood of children with names like Horsefly, Beanpole, and Fatty. These were the Vikings' slaves, the ones who toted firewood on their backs, cut peat from dank bogs, spread the fields with dung, and did the rest of the dirty work.

The many people held in thrall, or servitude, by the Vikings came from near and far. Some were Scandinavians themselves, who lost their freedom when they fell into debt or were con-

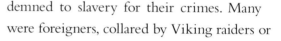

Viking women wore brooches like those at left, made of bronze, to fasten the shoulder straps of their gowns and to hold adornments such as the attached necklace and pendant.

demned to slavery for their crimes. Many were foreigners, collared by Viking raiders or traders and kept as their property or sold to the highest bidder at markets like the one at Hedeby. These thralls had no rights. They could marry, but any children they produced were slaves, as were the children fostered on slave women by their masters. When Vikings of high rank died, slaves might be sacrificed to serve them eternally in the next world. Anyone who killed a slave had to pay the owner compensation (the Vikings who settled in England set the value of a slave's life at eight cows). A small landowner with a dozen cows and a few horses might have three slaves; masters of large estates might have 30 or more. Rich or poor, a good husbandman took care of his slaves, as he did his animals.

Slaves lived side by side with their owners and were sometimes their concubines or kin. Motivated by family feeling or by gratitude for services rendered, some owners eventually freed their slaves or at least gave them a patch of land or training in a craft so that they could earn enough money to buy their freedom. Freed slaves looked for patronage and protection to their former owners and owed them fealty—an obligation passed on to future generations.

Freedom was infinitely preferable to thralldom, as the next stop of the god Rig on his legendary journey made clear. Having fathered the slave race, Rig proceeded to a comfortable hall, or farmhouse, where he enjoyed the hospitality of an industrious couple named Afi and Amma, or Grandfather and Grandmother. Grandfather, sporting a snug hip-length tunic called a kirtle and a neatly trimmed beard, was whittling wood by the fire, while Grandmother sat beside him spinning yarn, with a snood veiling her hair in modest fashion and brooches at her shoulders clasping her apronlike dress. They offered Rig a hearty meal and made room for him afterward in their bed. As before, Rig slept between his hosts for three nights before departing.

Nine months later Grandmother gave birth to a boy called Karl, or "Freeman." He was strong and ruddy cheeked, with bright, sparkling eyes. When Karl came of age, he married a comely girl with a fine goatskin cape and keys dan-

A pendant portrays a Norse woman with large beads hanging from a brooch at her shoulder. As shown here, a shawl often covered a woman's gown, which in turn was worn over a pleated linen shift.

gling from her belt—proof that she was prepared to be mistress of a household and take charge of it in her husband's absence. Their sons were named Strongbeard, Holder, and Smith, and their daughters Prettyface, Maiden, and Capable. These were the diligent men and women who owned and worked the farms, built the houses and barns, harnessed the oxen, milked the cows and churned the butter, and spun and wove the wool.

They had to be strong and capable, for they depended largely on their own resources. Villages in Scandinavia were few and far between, and they were small compared with the towns of Christian Europe. Most farms sat alone on narrow green coastal strips between the mountains and the sea. These free households, linked to their near or distant neighbors by communal ties and duties, formed the backbone of the Viking world.

Each farm served as its own tiny hamlet for an extended family and perhaps a few slaves. At its center stood the communal residence—a longhouse constructed more for warmth than for beauty, with walls made of wood, or sometimes sod or wattle and daub (wickerwork plastered with clay). Grouped around the longhouse, and sometimes attached to it, were various outbuildings—stables for livestock, storage sheds for food, workshops for forging iron and other crafts, boathouses for sheltering vessels in winter, and huts for storing other precious equipment like plows, fishing tackle, carts, sleighs, and skis. Some Viking farms had freestanding privies and saunalike bathhouses. Many homesteads were dotted with burial mounds, for Vikings felt that the dead should rest near their descendants.

Life in the longhouse was close and sometimes stifling. People moved about in a shadowy haze, for the building was usually windowless and the smoke hole in the roof failed to disperse all the fumes from the hearth fire or from the lamps with their acrid fish or whale oil. The interior was essentially one long hall, affording little in the way of privacy. At one end the master and his wife might have a sleeping area set off by a wooden partition, or they might be lucky enough to have a snug bed-closet, with a door that

The housewife also spent hours on end at her upright loom, fashioning the soft linen shifts, shirts, and trousers that often formed the first layer of clothing for the Vikings, and the warm woolen kirtles, cloaks, or shawls they wore on top. Such tasks, along with sewing and embroidery, brought a woman great credit and formed part of her legacy. One young Norwegian woman named Astrid was celebrated on a memorial stone as "the handiest maid in Hadeland." Another such monument in Sweden offered this tribute from a farmer to his wife: "A better housewife will never come to Hassmyra to run the farm."

The mistress of the house carried with her the tokens of her industry and authority. Dangling on chains from her brooches were her needles, her scissors, and her knife. Hanging from a cord around her waist were the keys to trunks or chests that held household ar-

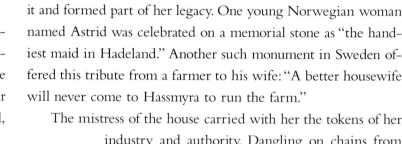

"Let whoever opens a door make certain there are no enemies hiding behind it."

could be closed and locked. But the rest of the household bunked down on the floor or on the long benches that lined the walls. During the day that dingy common space served as their kitchen, dining hall, and work area.

The mistress of the house was responsible for preparing and serving the food. She and her daughters milked the cows and goats; made cheese; brewed ale and honey-sweetened mead; ground grain in hand mills made of soapstone, called querns; cooked up the porridge that often served as breakfast; and prepared fish or meat for dinner by spit-roasting it, baking it amid glowing embers in the hearth, or boiling it by dropping hot stones into a pot of water well seasoned with juniper berries, mustard seed, or garlic.

ticles of special value entrusted to her care. Like her husband, she trod softly in leather shoes that resembled slippers, but with her various tools and with the jewelry that adorned her neck and arms, she jingled richly as she walked.

Marriage brought a Viking woman various assets. Her husband acknowledged her worth beforehand by agreeing to pay a bride price for her. After the simple wedding ceremony, marked by the drinking of "bridal ale," he often gave her a handsome gift. And if the marriage ended in divorce, he had to repay the dowry her father entrusted to him. Either partner could obtain a divorce, simply by announcing it in front of witnesses. A wife might put up with her husband's intimacies with a slave girl or concubine, but other lapses were harder for her to forgive. Women in Norse

In the interior of a reconstructed Viking dwelling in the Danish market town of Hedeby, an iron pot hangs over the hearth near an upright loom that was used by the mistress of the house to weave cloth. Although homes in towns like Hedeby were relatively compact, the typical Norse lodge was a longhouse like the replica at right, situated on the Swedish island of Gotland.

31

sagas were known to divorce their husbands for such failings as impotence or wearing "effeminate" clothing, and few things exasperated them more than signs of weakness or cowardice in their men. After all, the fortunes of the household were as much the wife's concern as her husband's, and if he failed to defend the family's welfare or honor, she counseled him to take forceful action or live without her.

Most Viking men were more than willing to start feuds or go off raiding when they had the chance. Unlike the dedicated fighting men who gathered around kings like Harald, however, the typical *karl* was limited by his many farm tasks to the role of a part-time adventurer. From fall through spring he usually had his hands full at home. Winter came early, and the months preceding it were devoted to harvesting and haymaking—a crucial task in this harsh clime, where a herd of 20 cattle required more than 50 tons of hay if it was to survive the long dark months of cold and snow. Gathering, drying, and storing that much fodder could keep 10 men laboring 10 hours a day for a month. And there were horses and sheep to be fed as well. When the hay was in, the men and boys rounded up the animals in their high mountain pastures and drove them home. The strongest of the livestock went into the barn. The rest were slaughtered, dried, and salted.

All through the fall the menfolk filled any spare hours they had by fishing and hunting, pursuits they continued in the winter by donning skis or skates. When the last of the snow finally melted around mid-April, the freemen and their slaves began to turn up the cold earth, plowing, spading, breaking up clods with hammers, and hauling out manure on sledges from the barns. The Vikings could not cultivate wheat so far north. Instead, they planted rye for bread, oats for porridge and feeding to the horses, barley for fermenting into ale, and flax for weaving into linen. In spring, too, they led or carried their half-starved cattle—some too weak to walk—from the barns to the near pastures, where the animals browsed until they were strong enough to be driven up into the mountains. That would be done amid other chores in early summer, when birds' eggs were culled from cliffside nests and lambs were weaned.

In high summer the tasks of the farm grew lighter and could be safely relegated to youngsters and slaves, under the supervision of the mistress. At last the men were free to venture. Some of the prospects that lured them away from home in these days of fair sailing and near-perpetual daylight were peaceful. Many farmers had goods to barter and set

With his mighty sword, King Olaf Tryggvason of Norway slays a sea ogress in a depiction of one of the many colorful legends related by Viking poets. Kings usually loomed large in such tales because poets were dependent on them for support and thus sang their praises.

time by themselves regarded with suspicion all those beyond their threshold. In the words of a Norse proverb, "Let whoever opens a door make certain there are no enemies hiding behind it." Even neighbors and in-laws might easily become enemies. It took little to start a quarrel—a spat over a stray animal, perhaps, or a perceived insult. The aggrieved party might then exact vengeance, not necessarily on the offender but on someone in his family. After that, the feud often escalated, leaving houses in embers and mothers in mourning. Before both families were utterly ruined, however, wiser heads sometimes prevailed and submitted the dispute for settlement, either to respected men who served as arbitrators or to the entire assembly. The resulting hearing was really just another test of strength for the rival families. An accuser would appear, supported by oath helpers who swore that they believed his accusation. The defendant might then summon his own oath helpers. To test their oaths, one party or the other sometimes underwent an ordeal, such as snatching a stone from boiling water. If the wound received healed cleanly, it was considered a sign of truthfulness. On occasion, the judges found nothing to choose between the two sides and ordered the principals to settle matters with a duel on neutral ground—an island, perhaps, or a crossroads. More often, one party was judged to be at fault and instructed to pay the other compensation, often in the form of wergild—or blood money—a penalty for the killing of a freeman that varied according to the status of the victim.

Not all offenses could be wiped out by the payment of compensation. Men found guilty of heinous offenses, such as murdering a freeman with whom one was not already engaged in a feud, might be outlawed, either for a set number of years or for life. The

off for the nearest trading town with soapstone from their local quarry, perhaps, or lengths of sailcloth that had been woven by their industrious wives.

Public assemblies were held in the summer as well, and all freemen in a given district or province were expected to attend. The main function of this local assembly, or *thing,* was to act as a court and resolve the stubborn disputes that arose with alarming frequency in the Viking homeland. Families who spent so much outlaw was banished and forfeited his property. If he failed to leave the country within a specified time, anyone who wished to do so could kill him with impunity.

Such measures might have done more to keep the Viking world at peace had it not been for the provocative role played by the chieftains, or jarls—the Norse equivalent of earls. Unlike the serfs of Christian Europe, the karls of Scandinavia owned their own land, but they still needed the protection of their local chieftains and were expected to defend the interests of those strongmen. Jarls who stood to gain or lose by the decision of an upcoming *thing* sometimes rallied their supporters and blocked the backers of a rival chieftain from reaching the council grounds. If someone close to a jarl was outlawed, he might place the culprit under his protection. Such maneuvers undermined the power of assemblies and fostered long and bloody conflicts between chieftains that helped condition Vikings for their fearsome assaults on foreigners. Often it was jarls who organized karls into fighting bands and hurled them in longships against enemies near and far.

According to Viking legend, the jarl was not simply a freeman whose ancestors had risen to a position of power by merit or luck. He was a breed apart, as distinct from karl as karl was from thrall. That, at least, was the moral of the last episode in the legend of Rig. After fathering the slaves and the freemen, that fruitful god wandered on until he came to a great hall, larger and finer than either of the houses he had slept in before. The door to that hall had a handsome ring on its handle, and the floor within was carpeted with rushes. Rig was greeted there by a man in his prime called Father, who was twisting a string for his bow beside an elegant woman called Mother, who sat admiring her fair arms and patting her sleeves. Mother spread a table with linen for Rig, and served poultry and pork, wine in silver bowls, and bread made of fine white wheat that only the wealthy could afford.

As was his custom, Rig stayed three nights and slept between the couple in their bed. Nine months

f   u   th

Inscribed within the figure of a snake, runes honor the memory of a young Swede who died far from home while seeking wealth and glory.

VIKING RUNES OF REMEMBRANCE

"Let no man carve runes to cast a spell," warned a Viking poet, "save first he learns to read them well." Vikings believed that runic inscriptions, carved on stone or other durable surfaces, were a potent gift from the gods that might indeed be used to cast spells—which could go awry, it was feared, if the author made a foolish error. But runes were prized above all as a way of paying tribute to those whose accomplishments might otherwise be forgotten.

The stone at left was one of 30 in Sweden that commemorated the casualties of an expedition led by a chieftain known as Ingvar the Far-Traveled to a place called Serkland. (Swedish Vikings ranged down through Russia to the Near East; Serkland may have been an Arab country.) The inscription praises the deceased in verse:

"Like men they traveled far for gold / And in the east they fed the eagle, / In the south they died, in Serkland." To "feed the eagle" meant to reduce enemies to carrion, so Ingvar's men must have claimed lives before losing their own.

Some runic inscriptions honored the deeds of the living. A silver neck ring plundered by Norwegian Vikings carried this tribute to their exploits in the Low Countries: "We paid a visit to the lads of Frisia / And we it was who split the spoils of battle." A Swede named Jarlabanki who built a causeway across a marsh in the 11th century proclaimed his good deed by erecting a group of rune-stones "in memory of himself in his own lifetime," as one inscription read. Since Jarlabanki was a Christian, the message ended with the words: "May God help his soul." Earlier Viking inscriptions invoked pagan deities: "May Thor hallow these runes."

Vikings of the ruling class were especially proud of their command of runes, but others mastered the letters as well. People who were less adept could leave a testament by hiring a professional carver like Opir of Sweden, who signed his name to more than 80 inscriptions. But whether they commissioned memorials or carved them themselves, Vikings used the runes to mark forever their connection with lost friends and kin. And sometimes the simplest were the most poignant, such as this message left by a Swedish Viking who buried his comrade along the Dnieper River in Russia: "Brand made this stone coffin for his partner Karl."

later Mother gave birth to a boy with fine hair and eyes as sharp as a snake's and swathed him in silk. The couple called him Jarl, and he grew expert in the ways of hunting and fighting. He was Rig's favorite child, and the god taught him runes—the Norse characters that the ancients used to convey their thoughts in writing and cast spells. Rig encouraged his son to claim his inheritance by challenging others for control of the land, and Jarl did just that, inciting war and staining the earth red. His conquests brought many farms and followers under his command and won him a fair wife named Lively.

With her, Jarl had 12 sons, all of them noble and fierce like their father. But the last of the 12 was the keenest of all, so precocious in battle and wise in runes that people likened him to Rig. This peerless

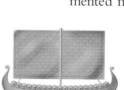

cloaking their silk tunics, golden bracelets encircling their bare arms, sparkling headbands binding their long hair, and torques and chains of beads ringing their necks. These were the king's gifts, and he saw to the needs of his men in other ways as well. The slave women who moved quietly among the benches were there to serve and sleep with them as they wished. And on the linen-covered trestle tables the women set mounds of food—garlicky beef or pork streaked generously with fat, dried fish smeared with butter, fine wheat bread, cheeses, and the fermented milk called skyr.

These select warriors came from good families. They might be the sons of jarls, sent to court to seal the bond between the chieftains and their overlord. Since early boyhood, they had conditioned them-

"Words of praise will not perish when a man wins fair fame."

lord was called young Kon, or *Kon ungr,* and his name came to mean king. He was the forerunner of Harald and others like him, who forged nations and regaled their followers at great feasts—rulers rich not only in land and weapons but in the runes and legends that ennobled the leaders of this warlike society and linked them to the gods.

Royal feasts took place in great halls, larger and more elaborate versions of the Viking longhouse, decked out to host the king's retinue. The wooden wall panels and posts were scrolled with carvings of coiled serpents or gripping beasts. Around the walls hung long, friezelike tapestries embroidered with scenes from myth and saga, their gold and silver threads glittering in the firelight. The king's warriors glittered, too, with lustrous furs

selves for warfare and hardship by climbing steep mountains and swimming in icy rivers and fjords. Weapons were their first toys, and constant practice made them experts with bow, sword, and spear. They yearned after glory, and longed for epitaphs like that of a Swedish warrior who fell in battle, "He kept on fighting while he could hold weapon."

They were bound together like brothers, and celebrated their ties in the great hall with fraternal drinking bouts. Women brought them vessels made from polished cow horns, embossed with silver and brimming with ale, mead, or rare wine imported from the south. These horns could not be set down, so they had to be drained dry or passed around, until everyone was intoxicated. Drunkenness was considered holy. It made the men feel brave and hearty. In its early stages, it sharpened their wits and helped them with the board games, riddles, and singing that they loved so much. It made the antics of the king's jesters and jugglers even funnier and the verses of his skalds sweeter. But as the feast wore on, men started to lose control of their tongues. As one skald warned pointedly:

Beer isn't such a blessing to men
as it's supposed to be;
the more you swallow, the less you stay
the master of your mind.

Those who drank too much might boast outrageously of their own feats and belittle the claims of their companions. It was all meant in sport, but the taunts stung and often led to blows. In the words of the same skald:

Even friends fond of each other
will fight at table;
nothing will ever bring to an end
the strife of men at meals.

With any luck, peacekeepers would intercede before blood was spilled and a feud blossomed. Perhaps the king's fools and poets were there in part to divert drunken warriors from such bickering. There was nothing better to heal rifts and bring the company back together in spirit than a good jest or a rousing tale of heroism, related by a skald whose verses conferred a kind of immortality on those who distinguished themselves in battle:

Cattle die, kinsmen die,
one day you die yourself;
but the words of praise will not perish
when a man wins fair fame.

It was an article of faith among Vikings that a brave warrior would be richly rewarded after death—and not just through the tributes of skalds. The noble fighting men who surrounded and served the king hoped that by dying gloriously in battle, they might win a seat in

Valhalla, the golden hall of the god Odin, patron deity not only of great warriors but of the rulers who retained them and the poets who sang their praises.

Odin belonged to a family of gods known as the Aesir, who dwelt in Asgard, a sort of heavenly fortress. (A separate family of gods known as the Vanir were associated with the earth—among them Frey and his sister Freya, who embodied the deep-rooted powers of fertility and desire.) Odin had mighty companions in Asgard, including the thunder god Thor, who struck flashes of lightning with his great hammer. But men of the warlike Viking aristocracy had a special reverence for Odin because he had braved terrible ordeals and claimed prizes that they could share. In one such exploit, Odin confronted a giant who lived at the root of the all-encompassing World Tree. Odin lost an eye in this daring venture, but it was a worthy sacrifice, for he drank from the spring of wisdom.

A GIFT FOR GAMESMANSHIP

Board games enlivened the nights that Vikings spent feasting together. The scene at left, portrayed on a Swedish rune-stone, shows a man holding a drinking horn while vying with his companion. In one such game, played on a square board, a player armed with 16 pieces tried to drive his opponent's king (below), defended by 8 pieces, into a corner.

Norsemen were sometimes buried with game pieces and made much of their skills. "At tables I play ably," boasted one noble Viking, who listed that as one of his nine talents, along with reading and writing runes, reciting poetry, playing the harp, skiing, rowing, making handicrafts, and shooting arrows.

Odin could grant warriors victory or send them to their deaths. But the noblest of those who perished joined him in Valhalla, where they feasted and boasted in much the same manner as they had on earth. They would not enjoy that reward eternally, however, for the Vikings knew that nothing lasted forever. The very fortress of the gods was vulnerable to attack. That was why Odin welcomed great warriors to his golden hall. He knew that he would need them in the struggle that was bound to come—the great reckoning known to the Vikings as Ragnarok, or the Doom of the Gods. Then all the evil in the world would be let loose, and the gods of Valhalla and their select warriors would engage in a cataclysmic struggle with the giants and beasts of the nether regions. Ultimately, the universe that began in frost would perish in fire. Yet a new world would emerge from the ashes, for the cycle of destruction and renewal was never ending.

The men in the king's hall understood all this and knew that to run from death was to forfeit their chance at enduring glory and to squander their reputation along with their vitality. A foolish man might try to prolong life's fleeting pleasures by shunning war, noted the skald, "but old age shows him no mercy, though the spears spare him."

For all their courage, the Vikings could also be shrewd and calculating and seldom risked their lives without a compelling reason or a decent chance at success. Among the heroes celebrated in Norse legend were some who held back from ventures they regarded as foolhardy or unfortunate. One such figure was Kveldulf, portrayed by Snorri Sturluson in *Egil's Saga,* an account of the tumultuous events that forced Snorri's Viking ancestors to flee Norway after Harald Fairhair rose to power. Kveldulf was a prosperous and independent-minded landowner who remained on his farm on the west coast of Norway and neither supported Harald in his campaigns nor opposed him. It was not a lack of daring that kept Kveldulf from fighting. "As a young man he used to go off on viking trips looking for plunder," Snorri noted. But he failed to see how his services could either help or hinder a man of Harald's might and luck, and he never committed himself without good cause.

Indeed, Kveldulf had a reputation as one of the most thoughtful men in his province. Neighbors sought his advice, and he always had wise words for them. They learned not to bother him toward evening, however, for when the shadows lengthened, a change came over him. He grew wary and sullen, and slunk off to bed. People called him Kveldulf, or "Evening Wolf," because he had the volatile nature of a shape changer—someone who turned wild in the dead of night or in times of danger. From the ranks of such shape changers came the fierce Viking warriors called berserks, or "bear shirts" (also referred to as "wolf skins"). At home, they might be considerate and soft-spoken, but when they went off to war and faced their enemies, they howled and bit their shields

but Thorolf was quick to accept, for he recognized that those who went along with Harald prospered, while those who defied him ended up dead or dispossessed.

For a time young Thorolf flourished in the king's service. At court, he befriended another of the king's men, called Bard, a princely figure from Ottar's homeland of Halogaland. Bard inherited from his father control of the mountainous interior and the right to trade with the Lapps and collect from them tribute—a portion of which went to the king. He was highly regarded by Harald and sat just four seats away from the king in his great hall. (Seated closest to Harald was his favorite retainer, the senior court poet.) Through Bard's influence and through his own winning ways, Thorolf soon gained a place among that elite group near Harald.

Thorolf's stature only increased when Bard

> ## "He had as many men with him as ever, and he lived in just as grand a style."

and fought with a snarling rage. Something of that dark fury entered Kveldulf at dusk.

Kveldulf bequeathed his somber character to his younger son, Skallagrim, a hard worker who shared his father's skepticism for reckless adventures and stayed close to home. Skallagrim's older brother Thorolf, by contrast, took after his spirited mother, "He was cheerful and generous, ambitious in all that he did and full of life." Skallagrim cared nothing for Harald Fairhair and his conquests, while Thorolf welcomed the king's rise as a golden opportunity. "I couldn't wish for anything better," Thorolf exulted when he learned from Kveldulf that Harald wanted one of the men of the family to join his company of warriors as a gesture of fealty. Kveldulf distrusted the summons and foresaw trouble,

died of wounds he sustained fighting for the king and left to Thorolf his land, his trading rights, and his wife. With the king's permission, Thorolf went north to take up those prizes. Yet the bequest turned out to be a mixed blessing, for Thorolf also inherited the hatred of two brothers who had been dispossessed by Bard's father and coveted the wealth of Halogaland. They sought out Harald and slandered Thorolf by claiming that he had murderous designs on the king.

Thorolf and his friends did their best to counter those false accusations by laying before Harald his full share of the Lapp tribute, including prize pelts of beaver and sable. But the slanderers assured Harald that for every three pelts Thorolf turned over, he kept thirty for himself. To test Thorolf's loyalty, Harald chal-

GUILE OF THE DRAGON SLAYER

In Viking legend, heroes mixed courage with cunning, as shown by the dragon slayer Sigurd. Young Sigurd was coaxed by his devious guardian Regin, a smith and sorcerer, into waylaying a dragon so that they could steal the beast's treasure. Wielding a sword forged by Regin, Sigurd killed the dragon *(right)*. As he sat roasting its heart while Regin slept, Sigurd scalded his thumb in the hot gore and thrust it in his mouth *(below)*.

With one taste of dragon's blood, he found he could understand the language of birds, who revealed that Regin planned to betray him. Sigurd acted quickly, lopping off Regin's head and claiming the treasure. The gold was cursed and brought him woe, but by outwitting Regin and striking first, Sigurd became a model for Vikings in their treacherous exploits.

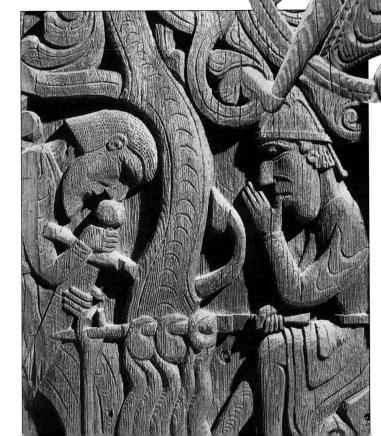

lenged him to relinquish the warriors he had gathered around him in Halogaland and return to court as the king's own retainer. For Thorolf as for other ambitious Vikings, however, having freemen at one's service was an incomparable source of pride. "I'll never let go of my men," he vowed.

Enraged, Harald stripped him of his powers and entrusted Halogaland and the Lapp trade to the scheming brothers. Thorolf withdrew with his acquired wealth and his followers to his own home and hall at Sandnes, near the southern end of Halogaland. "He had as many men with him as ever," Snorri noted, "and he lived in just as grand a style."

A short time later Harald's men seized a trading ship belonging to Thorolf. Kveldulf warned Thorolf not to test his luck against Harald's and urged his son to go abroad and offer his services to some foreign king. Instead, Thorolf ignored this advice and sought revenge by plundering one of Harald's ships and slaughtering several of the men who had taken his own vessel. "I have a feeling that this is the last time we shall ever meet," Kveldulf said to his son with grim resignation in the wake of those attacks, which were sure to be avenged by the king. "It would have been more natural for you to outlive me. But I'm afraid that's not the way it is to be."

When it came to feuding, Vikings were not sticklers for fair play.

41

Harald wanted a quick end to Thorolf and saw no reason to give him a fighting chance. Approaching furtively in the night, the king and his warriors surrounded Thorolf's hall at Sandnes. Even the guards were inside that night drinking with the others, and no one raised an alarm. Amid their revelry, they heard a shrill chorus of war cries like the keening of wolves in the night and leaped for their weapons.

Harald let the women and children and others who had no place in a fight emerge unscathed, but he rejected Thorolf's request that he and his men be allowed to come out and face their foes in open battle. "Set fire to the house," the king ordered. "I've no intention of fighting these men and losing my own."

With the door tightly barred and smoke filling the hall, Thorolf's men pried a beam loose from the smoldering roof and rammed at one corner of the building until they broke through. Outside, they faced an even hotter test—an enemy host in overwhelming numbers—but there was no turning back, and they advanced boldly to their doom. Thorolf ran at the king and killed his standard-bearer before being cut down. Harald himself delivered the deathblow to Thorolf, then called an end to the slaughter. "I'll have no looting," he declared, "everything here is mine." Yet he felt none the richer for his victory. A king's true worth was measured in

men, and Thorolf was not to be replaced. "It's a great loss," the king finally conceded, "losing a man like him."

The feud did not end there, for Thorolf's death drew into the vendetta the very man who had foreseen the danger of challenging Harald and tried to avoid it. Kveldulf knew well that Thorolf had aggravated the dispute through his pride and impulsiveness, but he grieved for his son no less deeply. It seemed to Kveldulf that darkness had descended on his house for good, and he retreated to bed listlessly, as if he no longer had the shape changer's power to rouse himself to fury. His surviving son, Skallagrim, hated to see his father surrender to grief without putting up a fight and urged upon him the time-honored remedy. "Better for us to seek our revenge for Thorolf's killing," he counseled the old man.

The longing for atonement lodged in Kveldulf's sore heart and slowly revived him. Thorolf's precious life would have to be paid for, he concluded, if not in blood then in money. If Harald would admit that he had been wrong in heeding the slanders against Thorolf and would offer wergild, then the feud might be laid to rest. Kveldulf lacked the strength to journey to the court and speak with Harald himself, so he sent Skallagrim, who so distrusted the king that he took as his companions 11 of the toughest

Gravestones in the shape of ships may have served symbolically to transport the souls of the dead, whose cremated remains were buried in the outlines. Other Viking graves were marked by runestones like the one at right, decorated with a frightful mask and dedicated to a man who fell "when kings fought."

men he knew—loners, sons of witches, and others with a "touch of the uncanny" about them, as Snorri put it. When they reached Harald's great hall, a herald announced the arrival of a dozen men—if you could call them that, he added, "for they're built and shaped more like trolls than human beings."

Harald greeted Skallagrim with unwelcome words, inviting him to become one of the king's men. "Maybe I'll come to like the way you serve me so much that I'll give you compensation for your brother," the king proclaimed grandly, adding that Skallagrim would have to watch his step and avoid Thorolf's errors. Skallagrim replied bluntly that serving Harald had not brought Thorolf much luck, and that he was not so vain as to try to succeed where his brilliant brother had come to grief.

Skallagrim left Harald fuming and returned home convinced that he and his father would never be reconciled to the king. In effect, they were now outlaws and would have to leave Norway or face Harald's wrath. They had heard reports of a green and distant refuge for the king's enemies—the recently discovered Iceland—and they prepared to sail there with their family members. But they still pined for vengeance, and before they departed, fate presented them with their chance. As they loaded their holds for the long and uncertain journey ahead, a familiar vessel appeared offshore—the ship that had been stolen earlier from Thorolf, laden now with two young passengers dear to Harald, the sons of his deceased uncle Guthorm, whom the king had sent for, to raise as his own.

Skallagrim led one longship to the attack, and Kveldulf another. As they closed on their target and prepared to board, Kveldulf, an old man, roused himself for one last battle. Taking up his long, heavy halberd with its menacing pike, he felt the change come over him and fought with an unstoppable frenzy. He singled out for punishment Harald's right-hand man, Hallvard the Hard-Sailing, and brought his pike down on Hallvard's head with such force that it sliced through his helmet and lodged deep in his skull. Kveldulf gave his weapon a mighty tug, Snorri related, and "lifted Hallvard into the air and tossed him overboard."

Few of Harald's men survived the savage onslaught. Many jumped overboard and were claimed by the sea. Among those who drowned were Guthorm's blameless sons, one just age 10 and the other 12, and "both lads of great promise."

After the battle Kveldulf was spent. Shape changers and berserks were capable of anything while their frenzy lasted, Snorri explained, but when the power left them, they were frail and vulnerable. A short time later Kveldulf and Skallagrim put out to sea in separate ships with their followers and family members, but the old man grew weaker by the day and died before they reached their destination. With his last breath, he instructed his people to lay his body in a coffin and toss it in the sea. Perhaps the currents would carry his coffin to the country they were bound for. If so, he said, Skallagrim should build his homestead "close to the place where I come to land." And so it happened. In death, the father guided his son to a fresh beginning in a promising new land.

For Snorri, this saga of ruin and rebirth had special meaning because it was part of his inheritance. Skallagrim was the first of the family to reach Iceland, and his son, Egill Skallagrimsson, became a great skald and adventurer whose memory inspired his distant descendant, Snorri, to preserve the tales of his ancestors in writing. Yet this was more than the isolated chronicle of one family. The story of Kveldulf and his sons was part of the larger saga of the far-ranging Vikings, scattered abroad by fate or the pursuit of fortune. Some went to plunder in England or on the Continent and put down roots there. Others ventured all the way to the Mediterranean and skimmed the shores of Africa in their dragon-headed longships. But all carried with them a mixed cargo of hopes and dreads, prides and resentments, virtues and vices. Like Kveldulf, these volatile Vikings underwent transformations along the way—and changed the shape of the world around them.

GODS AND GIANTS

The Norse viewed the universe as a structure with three levels. At its center was the great ash tree, Yggdrasil, whose roots stretched into each level: Asgard, the fortress of the gods; Midgard, where humanity dwelt; and Niflheim, the icy, barren realm of death. The ocean encircled Midgard, and across its watery depths, frost giants, enemies of humans and gods, roamed the land of Jotunheim.

Myths about these gods, giants, and other spirits reflected the hardworking and hardfighting nature of the Viking people. They told of awesome figures with the qualities that were most valued in Viking-age society: wisdom, courage, fertility, and self-reliance, as well as a healthy dose of deceit, greed, lust, and cruelty. By heeding these cautionary tales, the Vikings hoped to be rewarded with success in both this life and the next.

In an 11th-century Norwegian carved-wood portal, swirling vines and boughs entwine in what is believed to be a representation of Yggdrasil, the World Tree.

ODIN, LORD OF THE SLAIN

Odin, known as the All-Father, helped fashion the earth, the sea, the sky, and humanity before embarking on an insatiable quest for knowledge. In exchange for a drink from the spring of wisdom that watered the roots of Yggdrasil, the god gave up an eye. To gain the ability to see into the future and cause misfortune and death, he became a master of the black arts of sorcery. Seeking the mystical power of the runes and the means to speak with the dead, Odin hung himself from the World Tree for nine agonizing days and nights. He also stole the gift of poetry from the giants, and his association with it ran so deep that his priests were known as songsmiths.

Odin was chief among the Aesir, one of the two tribes of deities worshiped by the Vikings. His most ardent followers were rulers and poets, aristocrats who admired his mystical attributes. But all Vikings sought favor from Odin when facing battle. Those who fought and died bravely earned a place in Valhalla, Odin's hall in Asgard. There they could spend the afterlife drinking, wenching, and fighting until the coming of Ragnarok, the apocalyptic battle heralding the end of the world. Then they would fight against the forces of evil alongside Odin, who, it was said, would lose his own life in this final conflict.

In a ninth-century Swedish stone carving, Odin rides his swift eight-legged horse, Sleipnir, who could carry the god between the realms of the living and the dead.

At the end of time, the wolf god Fenrir, a symbol of death and destruction, fulfills his destiny and devours Odin, whose raven companion still grips his shoulder.

*"I know that I hung
On the windswept tree
For nine whole nights. . . .
I grasped the runes,
Screaming I grasped them."*

GUARDIANS OF LIFE AND DEATH

Norse laboring in fields and tending their animals to provide for the harsh northern winters called on Frey, a deity of the Vanir tribe of fertility gods, to help them. Frey controlled the sunshine, the rain, and the bounty of the earth as well as the fertility of animals and people. His female counterpart and sister, Freya, commanded the vibrant forces of love and sexuality. Ironically, Freya was also a goddess of war and death, claiming half the warriors who fell in battle for her own. Odin received the others.

Death, in the universe of the Norse, stalked the deities as well as humanity, and not even the warrior god Odin, Lord of the Slain, could protect those he loved from it. A dire prophecy about Odin's beloved son Balder sent Frigg, Balder's mother, on a mission to save his life. Promise me, Frigg demanded of all the elements of creation, that you will never harm my son Balder. All gave her their oaths—all except one plant, mistletoe, whom Frigg dismissed as too young to be a threat.

Secure in their son's invincibility, neither Odin nor Frigg objected as the other gods playfully hurled objects at Balder. But the mischievous trickster Loki, offspring of the frost giants, fashioned a spear from a mistletoe branch and tricked Balder's blind brother into throwing it. With Loki's guiding hand, the spear struck home, killing Odin's son.

Small figurines from Viking-era Sweden represent Freya *(left)* and Frey *(right),* gods of sexual potency, fertility, and abundance. An important part of a couple's wedding ceremony involved a sacrifice to Frey.

"It is good to call upon [Frey] for fruitful seasons and for peace. . . . On [Freya] it is good to call upon in affairs of the heart."

Loki suffers a cruel punishment for masterminding Balder's death: With his own son's intestines, Loki has been bound to a rock where a serpent drips burning venom upon him *(left)*. Meanwhile Balder *(below)* must endure consignment to the realm of the inglorious dead until after the cataclysm of Ragnarok, when he will reign in a peaceful, reborn world.

THOR, FIERY PROTECTOR

Fiery eyed and red haired, Thor commanded the elements of wind and storm. As he rode the heavens in his goat-drawn chariot, thunder and lightning shook the earth. Despite these ferocious attributes, it was Thor who watched over both human beings and his fellow deities and fought the enemies of world order. Those enemies included the World Serpent, lying in wait within the ocean depths, and the terrifying frost giants of Jotunheim, embodiments of the forces of chaos.

One memorable encounter between Thor and a frost giant occurred when the giant Hrungnir arrived unexpectedly at the fortress of Asgard while Thor was away in the east. After consuming vast quantities of the gods' alcoholic mead, Hrungnir began to boast that he would

A bronze figurine from 10th-century Iceland shows Thor grasping his prized hammer, Mjollnir. Measuring only about two inches in height, this object may have been carried as a charm.

flatten Asgard and kill everyone except for the beauteous Freya and Thor's wife, Sif, whom he would carry off. The gods cried out for their protector, who swept home on a western wind with eyes ablaze, ready for action. In the battle that followed, Hrungnir picked up a tremendous whetstone and hurled it at his foe as Thor let fly with his great hammer, Mjollnir. The hammer blasted the whetstone into bits and flew straight on into Hrungnir's head, killing the giant where he stood.

The Norse clearly viewed the universe as a place of constant tension between the forces of order and chaos. Often at the mercy of natural phenomena and the perversity of human conduct, Scandinavian peasants, shipwrights, and artisans found Thor's role as guardian of heaven and earth strongly appealing. Simple folk often invoked the thunder god for protection from the Odin-worshiping nobility. The people saw Thor as strong and forthright, instead of fickle and mysterious like Odin. Not surprisingly, of all the ancient gods of Scandinavia, Thor was the one who was most widely worshiped.

"Thor presides over the air, and governs the thunder and lightning, the fair weather and crops."

On this 11th-century rune-stone, Thor has snagged the World Serpent with his fishing line but has pulled so fiercely on it that his foot went through the bottom of the boat.

Thor's hammer was a powerful symbol used to consecrate weddings and funerals, and hammer amulets, such as the simple one shown above, were worn to invoke the god's protection.

CHAPTER TWO

TAKING EUROPE BY STORM

Rows of warriors stand poised to attack in this stylized view of Norsemen reaching France in the ninth century, when an "endless stream of Vikings," in the words of one French monk, subjected the people to "massacre, burning, and plunderings." The medieval artist depicted the warriors with shields and chain mail of the sort used by Normans—Frenchmen of Norse ancestry who conquered England in 1066.

hey surged up the Seine River, Viking longships by the hundreds, bound for the fortified village of Paris and the fruitful country that lay beyond. By Christian reckoning, it was in the year of the Lord 885, but the faithful in Paris, then a small town on an island in the Seine, might have been forgiven for wondering if their God had forsaken them. No doubt they prayed fervently for deliverance from these pagan Vikings, notorious for their raids on churches and monasteries, and approaching now in unprecedented numbers. Yet as dawn broke on the 24th of November, Parisians awoke to find the enemy at their gates. According to the French monk Abbo of Fleury, who chronicled the attack a century or so after the event, the oncoming army consisted of 40,000 "ferocious adversaries," packed onto more than 700 ships, choking the Seine for "more than two leagues downstream." Parisians looking out from the battlements that morning could see no water at all, he claimed, only a fearful forest of masts.

Had the Vikings really been "wild beasts," as Abbo characterized them, bent on spilling the blood of "fathers, sons, and mothers," they should have attacked at once and offered the Parisians no quarter. In this as in many other campaigns, however, the Norse intruders looked for ways to gain their objectives without sapping their own strength or annihilating their enemies—who often proved more valuable to the Vikings alive than dead. In fact, Paris meant little to the oncoming force. There were other towns upstream for them to pillage and fertile countryside whose harvests would help sustain them through the winter. Perhaps they would settle down in this promising land, as Viking interlopers were doing elsewhere. But their progress up the Seine was blocked by two low bridges that connected the island citadel of Paris to either bank. Flanked by strong towers, those bridges would have to be stormed at great risk—unless the outnumbered Parisians could be induced to allow the invaders free passage.

The leader of these Vikings was a Danish chieftain named Sigfred. Most of his followers were probably Danes as well, but their ranks may have been swelled by adventurers from elsewhere in Scandinavia and from places around the British Isles that Vikings had occupied in recent years. Sigfred was evidently a man of the world, wise in the ways of Christian Europe. With diplomatic guile, he sought out the abbot Joscelin, spiritual guardian of Paris, and urged him to yield, if only for the sake of his followers. "Oh, Joscelin, have pity on your self and on the flock entrusted to your care," he implored the bishop. "For your own good listen to what I have to say. We ask only that you let us pass beyond your city; we shall not touch it."

Bishop Joscelin—who shared authority over Paris with Count Eudes—explained to Sigfred that the Parisians were under a solemn obligation to oppose the Viking advance. They had been instructed to hold the city and its bridges by their king, Charles the Fat, a descendant of Charlemagne, whose great Carolingian empire had fractured since his death in 814. Although the West Frankish kingdom inherited by Charles the

Normandy derived its name from the Norsemen, who first raided towns and holy places along its rugged coast *(above)* around the year 800 and soon began venturing aggressively up the Seine River and other inlets. In 845 Vikings in longships launched an attack on Paris, portrayed at right by a 19th-century French artist. The town looked much the same when a larger Viking force laid siege to it in 885.

Fat encompassed only part of present-day France and Belgium, Joscelin told Sigfred that it extended "almost over the entire earth under the authority of the Lord, King and Master of the powerful. The kingdom must not allow itself to be destroyed; she must be saved by our city."

What would Sigfred think of himself if he were charged with just such a responsibility, Joscelin added plaintively, and were to concede without a fight? "My sword would be disgraced and unworthy of my command," Sigfred admitted. "Nevertheless, if you do not grant my request, I must tell you that our instruments of war will send you poisoned arrows at daybreak, and at day's end there will be hunger. And so it will be; we will not cease."

At dawn the next day, a French force consisting of no more than "200 brave warriors," by Abbo's reckoning, looked down nervously from the towers guarding the Paris bridges at a great Viking throng, advancing by land and by water with bows, spears, and slings in hand. All at once, the air was alive with missiles. "Stones smashed noisily onto painted shields," wrote Abbo. "Bucklers groaned and helmets grated under the hail of arrows." Surging toward the towers, the attackers began to hack at the walls with iron picks, but the defenders made them pay for their effrontery by pouring down boiling

This representation of a Viking with neat mustache, beard, and hair, capped by a traditional conical helmet with protective nosepiece, belies the stereotype of Vikings as unkempt savages. The figure, shown here at several times its actual size, was carved from elk horn.

oil and flaming pitch that singed the hair off the scalps of Vikings and sent them tumbling into the river in agony. The Parisians threw everything they had into the fight—including a large cartwheel, which crushed at least a half-dozen Danes below.

The hottest fighting occurred around the squat tower on the north bank, which the Vikings dubbed the "oven." Abbo noted that many Norsemen were carried away from there burned and bloodied, and died a short time later in the arms of the women who had joined them on this perilous venture. "Where have you come from?" wives cried to their fallen husbands. "From the oven?" Viking raids did not routinely include women. Their presence here suggests that the invaders meant to occupy this country for some time, if not permanently.

By day's end, portions of Paris were ablaze and the sky was aglow, but the towers had withstood the assault. When further battering failed to shatter the defenses, the Vikings cut their losses and settled down for a siege. Two months later, in January of 886, Sigfred's forces launched another assault, setting three ships alight and launching them upriver against the south bridge, only to watch in dismay as the burning hulks flickered out against the stone piers. Parisians took heart and paraded the bones of Saint Germain, a former bishop of Paris, around the ramparts to proclaim the power of their faith.

In early February, however, a flood carried away one of the bridges. Some of the Vikings slipped through in their longships, while others remained behind to maintain their stranglehold on the town, where famine and disease were taking a grim toll. Finally, nearly a year after the siege began, the sluggish King Charles reached Paris at the head of an army to break the siege. After a show of strength, however, he cut a deal with them, granting them free passage upriver—the very thing Joscelin and his fellow Parisians had so valiantly opposed—if Sigfred and his followers would content themselves with a winter's worth of pillaging and retreat the following spring. To seal the bargain, he promised the Vikings 700 pounds of silver as a parting gift.

Parisians were outraged by the pact and glad to see Charles deposed and Count Eudes installed as king in his place. The change mattered little to the Vikings, however. They received their 700 pounds of silver, as promised, and eventually withdrew with that and the other booty they had amassed back down the Seine toward the coast, where they found the prospects for settlement more favorable.

Far from feeling defeated, they had reason to regard this expedition as a success, for their goals were simpler and less sweeping than their foes imagined. They had no grand ambition to subjugate Europe or destroy Christian civilization. What lured them up rivers and inlets in longships was a lust not for blood but for bounty in the form of silver, gold, or good green land. To secure those gains, they were willing to bargain with their enemies and even prepared to adopt their ways. Indeed, some of the Vikings who marauded in France under warlords like Sigfred settled down in time along the lower Seine River and environs, embraced French customs and the Christian faith—and evolved

from Norsemen into Normans. True to their origins, these assimilated Vikings would remain a bold and assertive people, but their future conquests would be carried out for the glory of God and their adopted Normandy.

When Viking warriors first descended on Christian Europe in their longships, it scarcely seemed possible that they would ever come to terms with their foes and adopt their faith. The earliest recorded Viking raid on a Christian sanctuary, which took place in 793, devastated the monastery at Lindisfarne, off the east coast of England, and left such bitter memories that an English monk named Simeon of Durham still quivered with indignation when he described the attack some three centuries later. "The pagans from the northern regions came with a naval force to Britain like stinging hornets and spread on all sides like fearful wolves," he wrote. "They came to the church of Lindis-

Helmeted Viking warriors wearing trousers and carrying round shields touch swords on this picture stone from the island of Gotland, off the coast of Sweden. Unlike rune-stones, such monuments used images alone to commemorate the deeds of heroes and mythological figures.

farne, laid everything waste with grievous plundering, trampled the holy places with polluted steps, dug up the altars and seized all the treasures of the holy church. They killed some of the brothers, took some away with them in fetters, many they drove out, naked and loaded with insults, some they drowned in the sea."

This shocking onslaught was followed in years to come by similar raids on other exposed holy places along the coast of the British Isles and the Continent. Such blistering attacks from across the sea—which seemed almost supernatural at a time when few ships ventured far from land—fostered the impression that the Norsemen were a demonic force, bent on scourging Christians and defiling their sanctuaries. The cleric and scholar Alcuin, who served in the court of Charlemagne, denounced the attackers as heathens who "trampled the bodies of saints in God's temple like animal dung in the streets."

In truth, the Vikings bore no particular grudge toward Christianity. At least one Christian missionary had already visited Denmark in the early eighth century, and a bold German monk named Ansgar would proselytize at length in Scandinavia during the ninth century without meeting with martyrdom. The Vikings who raided Lindisfarne and other coastal monasteries simply coveted the

Among the treasure that Viking raiders buried was this spectacular hoard unearthed in Norway. It included a necklace of glass beads and other glittering ornaments, golden bracelets and neckbands, a delicate trefoil brooch, and coins from as far away as Arabia, made into pendants.

treasures that were stored there, including golden crucifixes and gospels encrusted with gems. And those targets were all the more tempting because the monks were such easy prey. Unhindered by the code that kept Christian marauders from attacking such defenseless holy places, the Vikings slaughtered some of the monks and carried off others as slaves along with the rest of their plunder.

Over the years the Viking raids grew more ambitious and penetrating. At first the attacks were limited to island monasteries or coastal towns. By the early 800s, however, Viking warriors were ranging up rivers and estuaries in their shallow-draft longships. Eventually, bands of Norsemen took to spending the winter in promising spots to extend the raiding season and to exact a steady stream of tribute from the locals, who often paid the intruders handsomely to avert their wrath. In time some Vikings chose to settle down in the lands they preyed upon.

Although the paths of the various Scandinavian peoples sometimes overlapped, each claimed its own sphere abroad, as dictated by geography and other considerations. The Norwegians, as hungry for land as they were for treasure, ventured west to the Shetland and Orkney Islands and down around the north tip of Scotland to the Hebrides and Ireland, before colonizing distant Iceland in the late ninth century. The Swedes, lured largely by the prospect of silver, slaves, and other spoils, crossed the Baltic Sea to Russia and followed its rivers deep into the interior to raid, trade, and establish bases from which they controlled parts of the Slavic hinter-

Rapacious warriors raise their weapons menacingly on this memorial stone erected at Lindisfarne after the monastery there was sacked in 793 by Viking raiders seeking treasure.

land. The Danes, as the most southerly of the Scandinavians, set their sights on the richest targets of all—the fertile and prosperous realms on either side of the English Channel. Those lands were also well settled and capable of stout resistance, however, and the Danes found that they could exploit them fully only by launching concerted campaigns like the one that nearly reduced Paris to rubble in 885.

In the decades preceding that expedition up the Seine, the energetic Danes came close to conquering all of England. By 850 they were wintering there, and by 866 Danish chieftains such as Guthrum and Ivar the Boneless were campaigning in England with large bodies of warriors and claiming wide swaths of territory, thus satisfying their ambitions abroad while their Danish homeland was coalescing slowly and painfully into a nation. In Denmark as in Norway, unification of the country under one king forced other proud and ambitious men to knuckle under or look elsewhere for fiefdoms to rule. Commanders like Guthrum who targeted foreign lands had no trouble recruiting followers, for the population was increasing substantially in all the Scandinavian countries and there were plenty of ambitious young men at loose ends, ready for any venture that would bring them the chance to acquire loot or land.

Some of those expeditions also included women, although they were not all of Viking origin. During the winter of 873-874, for example, nearly one-fifth of those occupying a Danish military camp near the English town of Repton were women. Judging by the remains of those who died there, however, the women were probably English rather than Scandinavian. Some may have chosen to consort with the Vikings, for the Anglo-Saxons were divided in their loyalties. As yet, no overlord had emerged who was capable of uniting the various kingdoms of England, and rivalries between neighboring realms provided openings for the Danes.

To claim control of the English interior, the invaders had to

Danish warriors under the command of Ivar the Boneless come ashore on England's southeast coast in 866 in this illustration from an 12th-century English chronicle.

THE VIKINGS INVADE BRITAIN

The Vikings who descended on England left a fearsome impression, and none more so than a lanky Dane known as Ivar the Boneless. A much tougher adversary than his name implied, Ivar honed his predatory skills in Ireland before mustering a horde of warriors and assailing the Anglo-Saxons, who were weakened by disputes among their petty kings and seemingly ripe for conquest.

Ivar was one of several allied Viking chieftains who invaded England beginning around 865 and made up a "great heathen host," as the contemporary record called the Anglo-Saxon Chronicle put it. Some in their path tried to buy them off, the chroniclers noted, but the Danes did not always honor the bargain, sometimes plundering the very people who had bribed them for peace.

Not content just to pillage, Ivar and his henchmen claimed territory and toppled rulers. In 869 his men earned lasting noto-

riety by seizing and executing Edmund, king of East Anglia *(right).* A year later, amid mounting opposition, Ivar returned to Ireland, leaving it to others to reckon with the resistance such harsh measures had provoked. Long after the Danes came to terms with the Anglo-Saxons, the depredations of Ivar and his kind continued to be vividly portrayed by English artists and chroniclers.

Edmund looks to heaven as Ivar's men pierce him with arrows. One account likened Edmund to a sea urchin "closely set with quills."

An English monk leads a cart loaded with sacred relics over a bridge, hoping to escape the Danes.

modify their tactics. Although they preferred to attack by ship, the Danes adapted to the challenges of land warfare by marauding on horseback along the enduring network of Roman roads, dismounting to fight on foot only when their victims dared to put up a fight. The English were hard-pressed to resist, given their political divisions and their lack of anything resembling an army. When the two sides did clash, there was plenty of cruelty on both sides. In 869 the Danes made a martyr of Edmund, the king of East Anglia, by tying him to a tree and skewering him with arrows. A band of English peasants, for their part, flayed some captured Danes and tacked their skins as trophies to the door of a church.

It remained for Alfred the Great, of Wessex—the same king who later welcomed the Norwegian merchant Ottar to his court—to translate seething hostility toward the Viking intruders into cogent opposition. A ruler of keen intellect, Alfred owed his success not simply to his military prowess but to his bargaining skills. Many a leader purchased a dubious peace from the Danes by agreeing to pay them steep tribute, known as Danegeld, which left the local populace overtaxed, demoralized, and vulnerable to future attacks. Alfred was loath to offer any such concessions, however, even after a Danish army led by Guthrum overran his kingdom in 878. Instead, he rallied his supporters and forced the invaders to accept a pact that left him in firm command of his native Wessex and neighboring Mercia.

The deal was not without compensations for Guthrum and his fellow Danes. By its terms, they formally retained control of a large area north and east of a line that cut diagonally across England from the mouth of the Thames River to the Irish Sea. Known as the Danelaw because it fell under Danish authority, that area encompassed some 25,000 square miles and became one of the largest and most fertile grounds for Viking settlement outside Scandinavia. In accepting the deal, however, Guthrum made a concession that proved prophetic for those who flocked to the Danelaw and intermingled with the locals: He underwent baptism and recognized Alfred as his godfather. Guthrum did so as part of his bargain with Alfred and probably remained something of a pagan at heart, loyal to

VIKING-AGE YORK

After occupying the English town of York, Danes transformed it into a Viking settlement called Jorvik *(above)*, filled with timber buildings with thatched roofs and wooden walkways that led down to the riverside docks.

A thriving trade center, Jorvik was home to all sorts of artisans, who toiled in dimly lit one-room houses producing wooden cups and bowls; ornate jewelry of amber, silver, and gold; and clothing made from wool. A woolen sock *(left)*, sewn with a single needle and plied yarn, was made by a local weaver.

Odin and other gods in the Viking pantheon. But his conversion signaled that here, as in Normandy, Vikings and their descendants would ultimately become dutiful members of the Christian society they once pillaged and profaned.

While Danes were battling for control of England, Norwegians were embroiled in struggles of their own with the stubborn Gaels they intruded upon in Ireland. Those conflicts would forever be cloaked in legend, for both sides were given to spinning imaginative yarns from the raw stuff of history. Irish lore told of a sinister Norwegian chieftain named Thorgils, or Turgeis, who invaded Ulster around the year 840 with 10,000 warriors in more than 100 longships and sacked the treasure-laden monastery at Armagh, the shrine of Saint Patrick. There Thorgils set himself up as a pagan high priest, joined by his wife Ota, or Aud, who was something of a sorceress herself, given to chanting spells.

Not content with desecrating Christian holy places, Thorgils and his marauders reportedly transformed the altars into heathen shrines and seduced a wayward Irish faction known as the Gall-Gaedhil, or Foreign Gaels, into renouncing Christianity and joining the pagan rites. The whole country might have fallen under Thorgils's evil spell had not the ruler of one Irish realm, the king of Meath, used some craft of his own and sent his daughter and 15 warriors disguised as maidens to lure Thorgils and his love-starved captains to a rendezvous beside a lake, where the Norwegians were overpowered and drowned.

This fanciful tale contained a kernel of truth. Vikings seldom imposed their rituals on the people they conquered, but in Ireland, as in Scotland and other places Vikings ventured, there were local people like the so-called Foreign Gaels who willingly trafficked and intermarried with the intruders and found their pagan rituals more congenial than Christian sacraments. There were also many others like the king of Meath who despised the Vikings and would try any trick to be rid of them.

By all evidence, Ireland in the ninth century was a fiercely contentious place. Not long after Norwegians established themselves there in force and founded the town of Dublin as a military base and trading center, Danes butted in and vied with their fellow Scandinavians for dominance. That struggle was resolved at least temporarily in 853, when a large fleet arrived in Ireland led by a Norwegian warlord named Olaf, who sent the Danes packing. From Dublin, Olaf and his henchmen launched expeditions to subdue the restive Irish and carve out fiefdoms in Scotland. Resistance remained strong, however, and eventually the Norse intruders were either ousted or assimilated, and Ireland and Scotland reverted to local control. Only on desolate islands like the Orkneys and distant Iceland did the Norwegians establish enduring colonies.

Like other dramatic events in Norwegian history, the tumultuous ventures to Ireland and Scotland were evoked in Icelandic sagas. One remarkable woman celebrated in saga summed up this chapter in the odyssey of her people. Known as Aud the Deep-Minded, or Aud the Deeply Wealthy, she possessed a keen wit and made the most of the fortune she inherited. Her father, Ketil Flat-Nose, was among the chieftains displaced from Norway by the rise to power of King Harald Fairhair in the late ninth century. Unwilling to bow to Harald, Ketil recognized that he and his kin had only two choices: "to flee the country, or else be killed off each in his own place." Ketil resolved "to go west across the sea to Scotland," the saga related. "He knew the country well, for he had raided there extensively."

When her father emigrated, Aud was already living abroad, having married a fierce and far-ranging Viking named Olaf the White and having accompanied him to Ireland, where he reportedly "took over Dublin and the region dependent on it and became king there." (His exploits in fact bore a close resemblance to those of the Olaf described in Irish accounts, who ousted the Danes.) Olaf the White ultimately died fighting the Irish, and

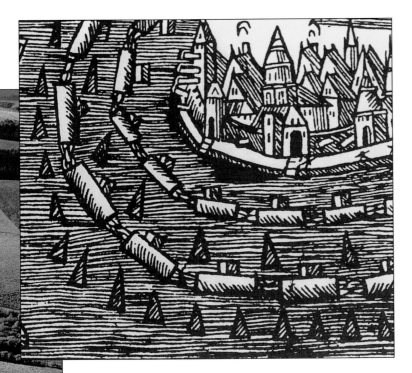

Aud sailed off with their son, Thorstein the Red, to the Hebrides, where her father had found refuge. When young Thorstein came of age, he went a-viking with a vengeance, raiding far and wide and claiming a kingdom for himself in Scotland. Aud joined him there at his great hall in Caithness, in the far north, only to see her son suffer the same fate as her husband—death at the hands of the feisty locals he presumed to rule over.

With Thorstein gone, Aud found herself in grave peril, but she proved to be a resourceful Viking in her own right. Hemmed in by hostile Scots at Caithness, she sent men furtively out into the forest to build a ship as swiftly as they could. When their work was done, they hauled the vessel down to the shingled shore, and Aud slipped off in the dead of night, taking with her all her valuables and something even more precious—her grandchildren, still grieving for their slain father. Last to clamber aboard the ship were 20 Viking warriors, loyal to the woman who now commanded the fortunes of the family. Ahead lay an epic journey that would carry Aud and company, step by step, from Caithness to the Orkneys to the Faeroes, and on to permanent refuge in Iceland, where Aud's fortitude would never be forgotten. "It would be hard to find another example of a woman escaping from such hazards with so much wealth and such a large retinue," concluded the saga. "From this it can be seen what a paragon amongst women she was."

Not content with celebrating their ventures to the northern islands, the expansive Norwegians even claimed part of the credit for conquering Normandy, a place occupied largely by Danes. According to the Icelander Snorri Sturluson in his *Heimskringla*—which related the exploits of Harald Fairhair and other Norwegian rulers—the Viking chieftain named Rollo, who founded Normandy, hailed from Norway; there he was known to his countrymen as Rolf the Ganger ("the Walker") because his girth was so great "that no horse could carry him." Just how

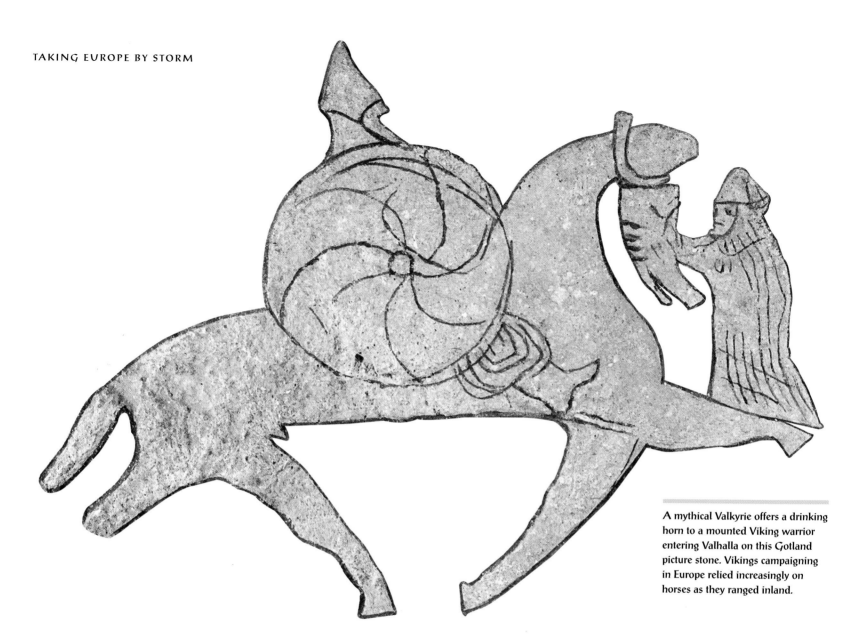

A mythical Valkyrie offers a drinking horn to a mounted Viking warrior entering Valhalla on this Gotland picture stone. Vikings campaigning in Europe relied increasingly on horses as they ranged inland.

this hulking Norwegian became the leader of the predominantly Danish force that seized Normandy was never explained, but it was not beyond the realm of possibility. Although Vikings of different nationalities sometimes vied for the spoils of conquest, as in Ireland, the Scandinavians were still one people by language and culture, and rulers from one country sometimes attracted followers from another.

Rolf the Ganger was the son of Rognvald, a Norwegian jarl who, unlike Aud's father Ketil, resolved his differences with Har-

ald Fairhair and became one of the king's most beloved and trusted men. Rognvald could do no wrong, as far as King Harald was concerned, but Rolf did not enjoy the same royal license. Harald had issued an edict forbidding "by the greatest punishment, any plundering within the bounds of the country," but young Rolf was no more able to hold in check his penchant for pillaging than he was able to ride a horse. After marauding abroad for a while, he headed back in high spirits and celebrated his return to Norway by conducting a *strandhögg*—a coastal raid for cattle and other property—the sort of thing that Scandinavians had been carrying out in their home waters for ages.

Perhaps Rolf felt that this hardly counted as plundering, but Harald was unforgiving. Observing proper legal form, he "assembled a thing," Snorri related, "and had Rolf declared an outlaw." Rolf's mother pleaded with the king to pardon her son, warning that Rolf, if treated like a mad wolf and "driven to the wild woods away / May make the king's best deer his prey." Wisely, however, Rolf chose not to become embroiled in a destructive feud with Harald. Instead, he lumbered off to distant parts, where he could plunder to his heart's content. He ended up in France, where he purportedly "subdued for himself a great earldom, which he peopled with Northmen, from which that land is called Normandy."

This formidable Viking chieftain was known to the French as Rollo, and whatever his origins, he played a crucial role in European history. In 911 Charles the Simple, then king of the West Franks, concluded that the Norsemen were so firmly established along the coast of France that there was no longer any point in fighting them. Charles cut a deal with their leader, granting him Normandy as his personal fiefdom. In return Rollo pledged to become a Christian and swore allegiance to the French king, promising to protect his kingdom from any further Viking depredations. Rollo sealed the bargain by marrying a French noblewoman.

Many of the Vikings who settled down in Normandy emulated their leader, taking French brides and converting to Christianity. Perhaps some went a step further and combined godliness with cleanliness, like the Danes in England, who reportedly bathed each Saturday and changed their woolens at regular intervals, the better to attract fastidious English wives. In any case, Norse customs and language soon began to die out in Normandy. A grandson of Rollo had to be sent away from the Norman capital at Rouen in order to learn the speech of his ancestors. Future Norman rulers would content themselves with mastery of the French language and scarcely give a thought to their Viking heritage.

While Danes and Norwegians were making a deep impression on western Europe, Swedes were pursuing mercenary ventures in the East that mingled raiding with trading and carried them from the shores of the Baltic all the way to the Black Sea and

This handsome stirrup inlaid with silver and copper was among the riding gear buried with a wealthy Viking who prided himself on his horsemanship.

the gates of Constantinople. In the process, these Rus—as Slavs referred to the Swedes—gave their name to Russia and forged links not only with the Byzantine Empire but with the rich Arab world as well. Indeed, it was Arab silver more than anything else that lured these Swedes deep into the heart of Russia and enriched their own homeland, transforming the market town of Birka, near modern-day Stockholm, into a place of great wealth and vitality.

The Swedes were not alone among Vikings in supplementing the prizes of conquest and plunder with the fruits of trade. The Norwegians in Ireland, for example, after founding Dublin and Cork as coastal forts, developed them as market towns and lured locals there to trade for goods imported by Viking merchant ships. The Danes did much the same after occupying York in England and Rouen in Normandy. At the same time, merchants and artisans back home were profiting by the Viking success abroad. Like Birka in Sweden, the Norwegian market town of Kaupang and the Danish trading center of Hedeby grew larger and livelier during the ninth century as the Vikings extended their range overseas.

Into those havens poured ships crowded with booty and slaves. In exchange, the market towns supplied outgoing merchant ships with Scandinavian articles that were coveted abroad, including furs and walrus ivory. They also hosted communities of artisans who transformed raw materials into alluring articles prized both by the Vikings and by their clients overseas. Hedeby, in particular, was a place where goods were both crafted and traded. There, behind a lofty rampart designed to protect this town filled with loot from itself being plundered, lay narrow, timbered streets lined with small, windowless workshops, where handy Vikings turned out horn combs, glass beads, weavings, pottery, sword hilts, and jewelry. In its heyday in the 10th century, Hedeby was a town as cosmopolitan as any in Europe, and the bustle of its open market and the music of the many languages on the streets must have been as alluring to visitors as the goods themselves.

Birka was perhaps an even richer place, judging by the quantities of Arab silver hoarded by merchants there and buried with the dead in the town's cemetery. It mattered little to the merchants in Birka what value was assigned to the coins they received. They gauged the worth of the money in weight on their scales. To settle accounts precisely, they some-

times hacked coins in two. Artisans in Birka crafted dazzling trophies for successful Vikings and their wives by adorning bracelets and necklaces with coins, crystals, gems, and other charms from distant lands the Norsemen visited. Among the other prize commodities purveyed in Birka were captives from Russia known as Slavs, rounded up in such prodigious numbers that their name became synonymous with the word *slavery* (although people from many other lands were enslaved by Vikings as well). Many of the Slavs the Swedes seized abroad were sold to Arab traders for silver, but there was always a surplus to offer at market back home to Vikings who needed more hands on the farm or extra serving women in their great halls.

Birka and all who visited there came under the protection of the Swedish king, who appointed a royal prefect to preside over the local thing and make certain that foreigners were treated fairly under the law. A Swede faced the same penalty for murdering a visiting Dane or German, for example, as he did for killing one of his own countrymen. The king insisted on such evenhandedness because he wanted foreign merchants to feel at home in Birka. After all, he had first pick of the newly arrived goods and used this privilege to ensure that his own household and retainers were the most lavishly appointed in the land.

Viking merchants used scales like the bronze set above to weigh silver and gold by balancing the precious metal against calibrated iron weights *(far left)*. To even the scales precisely, traders added fragments of coins that had been hacked up.

The midnight sun overwhelms the moon and stars in this Scandinavian market scene showing fur pelts hanging in a vendor's stall at right and a tradesman offering fine glassware in exchange for fish at left.

Birka may have been a fairly civilized place, but the Swedish ventures that filled its coffers with silver and other prizes were long, hard, and brutal. There were two main routes south through Russia. One followed the Dnieper River down to the Black Sea—at the far side of which lay Constantinople—and the other descended the Volga River to the Caspian Sea, the gateway to the Arab world. To reach the headwaters of the Dnieper or the Volga in central Russia, Swedes first had to traverse the Baltic and then make tortuous journeys inland that required them to trek overland between rivers. The vessels they used for

the purpose were considerably smaller than their usual longships. Described in contemporary accounts as dugouts, "made from a single trunk," some may have carried a small sail in order to supplement the power of oars when the wind was favorable, but the boats had to be light enough to be towed up rapids or portaged across land to the next waterway.

Some Swedes ventured all the way to Byzantium or the Arab world to trade or raid. The temptations of Constantinople proved particularly hard to resist, and more than once the Rus attempted to take by force the place they knew as Mikligardr, or the

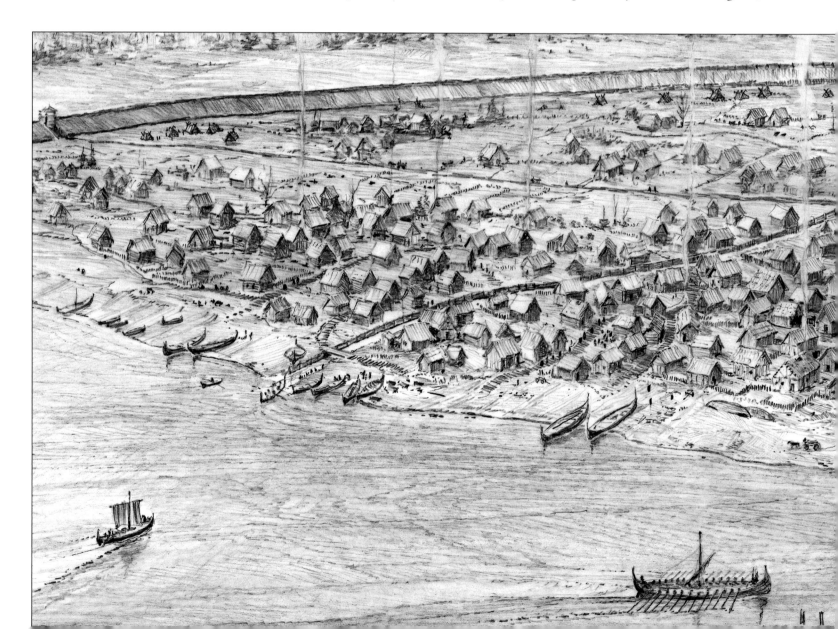

Great City. Around 907, according to a Byzantine account, tens of thousands of Rus attacked Constantinople by sea. The Byzantine emperor pressed for peace, agreeing to pay tribute to the Vikings and offering them trade concessions. Conflict between the two sides flared up anew in later years, and the Rus sacked many a Byzantine monastery and village. But such ferocity won them the grudging respect of the Byzantine emperors, and Swedes were soon prominent among the Vikings recruited to serve as soldiers of fortune in the Varangian guard, whose members protected the emperor's palace and pillaged his enemies.

The Rus did not have to travel to Byzantium or Baghdad to make a killing, because caravans from the south and east often met them halfway at trading centers such

The Danish trading center of Hedeby, girded by a rampart and crowded with merchant and artisan homes, was a bustling place in the Viking age of conquest, frequented by merchant vessels and warships laden with captured slaves and other prizes. Among those that ventured here was an Arab merchant who described it as lying "at the other end of the world sea."

as Bulgar, on the Volga River, and Kiev, on the Dnieper. Swedes flocked to such marketplaces and established bases there, from which they scoured surrounding areas for slaves and furs to offer in barter. They became so well established in Kiev that they were later credited with founding the town. Indeed, a Russian chronicle of the 12th century claimed improbably that the Rus, or Swedes, established Kiev as their capital by invitation of the native Slavs, who felt incapable of governing themselves. "Our country is rich and immense," they supposedly told the Rus, "but it is rent by disorder. Come and govern us and reign over us."

Whether they came to save the local Slavs or to exploit them, Swedes indeed dominated the Kiev area and other parts of Russia for some time before being ousted or assimilated like their Viking counterparts in western Europe. By the 11th century the rulers of Kiev no longer bore names like Rurik or Oleg and instead went by such Slavic titles as Vladimir and Yaroslav. In the heyday of the Rus, however, Russia was seemingly theirs to do with as they pleased, and they were not shy about it. In 922 an Arab traveler named Ibn Fadlan encountered them at Bulgar, and he set down in writing a lively and sometimes lurid account of these Vikings at their brashest, making themselves at home on foreign soil.

Ibn Fadlan was the secretary of a delegation from the caliph of Baghdad to the king of the Bulgars, a Turkish people who proved receptive to Islam. Their king remained in control of the marketplace at Bulgar despite the strong Viking presence, and Ibn Fadlan's delegation had come there to instruct the king in Muslim rites and to support construction of a permanent fort that would render Bulgar more secure. Among the precious goods that poured into Bulgar were silk from China and silver from Arabia, and Ibn Fadlan and company did not want to see the Rus or anyone else make free with the place and its treasures. For now, Norsemen, Arabs, and other visitors mingled warily but without undue hostility in the crowded streets, fetid with the stench of camels and other pack animals, whose hoofs churned the puddled earth into mud. Tattooed Rus with fat money belts haggled with caftaned merchants from Baghdad, while carts trundled by, groaning under loads of furs.

As a cultivated Muslim, Ibn Fadlan regarded the Rus he encountered at Bulgar as heathens and barbarians, but his account of their customs was honest and discerning, if not entirely impartial. Like many foreigners, Ibn Fadlan was impressed by the size and

Above, in a woodcut illustrating Viking ventures, a Swedish trader visiting Russia aims his bow at a squirrel, one of the many furbearing creatures whose pelts the Vikings offered, along with captured slaves, to merchants from the Middle East. At right, Viking traders in Russia haul their boat overland, a necessity when bypassing falls or rapids or trekking from one body of water to another.

swagger of the Vikings who lumbered down Bulgar's muddy lanes. "I have never seen more perfect physical specimens," he wrote, "tall as date palms, blonde and ruddy." Indeed, Vikings were on average several inches taller than the Europeans they traded and tangled with, and their stature was enhanced by their prominent weaponry and adornments. "Each man has an axe, a sword, and a knife and keeps each by him at all times," Ibn Fadlan remarked. No less imposing were the dark tattoos that covered them "from finger nails to neck," sinuous designs that looked to Ibn Fadlan like trees.

In other respects, however, the Arab observer found these Vikings less than impressive. "They are the filthiest of God's creatures," he reported. "They have no modesty in defecation and urination, . . . nor do they wash their hands after eating. They are thus like wild asses." When they bothered to cleanse themselves, they did so in what he deemed "the dirtiest and filthiest fashion possible." Each morning a female slave would present her master with a basin of water with which to rinse his hands, face, and hair. Having done so, he would then blow his nose and spit into the basin. "When he has finished," wrote Ibn Fadlan with revulsion, "the servant carries the basin to the next person, who does likewise." Apparently, sharing the same basin in this fashion was a mark of comradeship.

The Rus were not the only people Ibn Fadlan met with on his journey who violated the strict rules of cleanliness and propriety that he adhered to on religious grounds. As a Muslim, he washed regularly in running water to cleanse himself of the pollution associated with bodily functions. Vikings felt little shame about such matters, however. Communal living conditions in their longhouses back home did not incline them to modesty, and even such polite habits as relieving oneself in private had to be dispensed with when they were off on long voyages together.

The slaves that attended the Swedes were not the only women

At left, in a scene from a medieval Russian chronicle, Slavic subjects offer pelts as tribute to the Swedes, or Rus, who controlled Kiev by the late ninth century. Below, a Rus war fleet besieges Constantinople in the early 10th century, circumventing the great chain guarding the harbor there by wheeling their ships right up to the city gates—a tall tale that may have been inspired by the Viking practice of mounting ships on rollers so as to get around obstacles.

that accompanied them. As Ibn Fadlan picked his way among the tents and wooden huts of the Rus, he saw women he took to be their wives, decked out in precious ornaments. They wore "neck rings of silver and gold," he observed, with the number of rings varying according to the wealth of their husbands. Similarly, their status was signaled by the quality of the twin brooches they wore in Scandinavian style above either breast. Those with the richest husbands boasted brooches of silver or gold rather than iron. Some of these well-appointed women may have been Swedes who accompanied their husbands to Russia; others were perhaps favored concubines.

The Rus may have been infidels in Ibn Fadlan's eyes, but they were not without beliefs and rituals. In hopes of improving his trade, a Rus would lay offerings of food and drink before wooden idols and pray for the spirits

to send him a wealthy merchant, "who will buy from me whatever I wish and will not dispute anything I say." If his prayers were answered, the man slaughtered sheep and cattle, and placed the heads on stakes in thanksgiving before the altars, along with portions of the meat. "In the night, dogs come and eat all," Ibn Fadlan noted, "but the one who has made the offering says, 'Truly, my Lord is content with me and has consumed the present I brought him.' "

Ibn Fadlan also witnessed the spectacular cremation of a Rus chieftain, laid out on his ship and immolated along with a slave girl, sacrificed for the occasion. The ritual bore similarities to the ship burial at Oseberg of a great lady and her female retainer, although in this case the vessel and its occupants were burned before being covered over by a mound of earth. The cremation was preceded by 10 days of mourning, during which the chieftain's grieving friends and relatives quaffed an intoxicating brew Ibn Fadlan called *nabidh*. "They stupefy themselves by drinking this nabidh night and day," he wrote. "Sometimes one of them dies cup in hand."

The slave girl who was destined to be cremated along with the chieftain drank herself into a stupor as well, after first volunteering to be sacrificed. "Who among you will die with him?" the slaves were asked, and she replied obligingly, "I." She may have been fond of the dead chieftain, and she shared the belief that he was bound for a glorious place in the next world and chose to accompany him. Placed in the care of two women who never let her out of their sight, she drank and sang blissfully, as if looking forward to her ultimate reward.

The victim was treated like the intended bride of the deceased, but she was not expected to hold herself in reserve for him. Before being put to death, she visited the tents of several men close to the chieftain and had intercourse with them. "Tell your lord I have done this out of love for him," each man told her as she departed. Then she was led to a structure resembling a door—a symbolic barrier between this world and the next—and was lifted up three times by men who cradled her feet in their palms. With each successive lift, she told of seeing her father and mother on the other side, other relatives dear to her who had passed away, and finally her deceased master, awaiting her in a green and beautiful paradise. "He calls me," she announced; "take me to him."

The mourners obliged by conducting her to the ship, placed onshore atop a mound of kindling. Her master had been laid out there in a pavilion on deck. By now, his corpse had "grown black from the cold of the country," Ibn Fadlan noted, but he was dressed in fresh finery, including furs and a "caftan of brocade with gold buttons," and propped up with cushions amid fruits, fragrant plants, weaponry, and the butchered bodies of a dog, two horses, two cows, a rooster, and a hen. As the victim approached the pavilion, she was met by an old woman called the Angel of Death, who encouraged her to drink a final cup of nabidh before meeting her fate.

At the last moment the victim appeared to waver, but the Angel of Death seized her by the head and forced her into the pavilion, where the ceremony reached its grim conclusion. As warriors beat their shields with sticks to muffle her cries, Ibn Fadlan related, "six men went into the pavilion and laid her at the side of her master." Two men held her feet and two grasped her hands, while the Angel of Death looped a cord around her neck and gave the crossed ends to the other two men for them to pull. Then the old woman seized a broad-bladed dagger and plunged it repeatedly between the victim's ribs, and the men tightened the cord "until she was dead."

Afterward the dead chieftain's closest male relative cast off his clothing and approached the pyre naked with torch in hand and set the kindling alight. Swiftly, flames engulfed "the ship, the pavilion, the man, the girl and everything in the ship," Ibn Fadlan wrote. "A powerful, fearful wind began to blow so that the flames became fiercer and more intense." Soon, nothing remained but cinders and ashes.

As the fire died down, a Rus who was standing beside Ibn Fadlan spoke to him bluntly through an interpreter. "You Arabs are fools," he commented. "You take the people who are most dear to you and whom you honor most and you put them in the ground where insects and worms devour them. We burn him in a moment, so that he enters Paradise at once." Then the Rus startled his Arab companion by laughing ecstatically.

Among the most exotic foreign treasures ever obtained by Vikings was this miniature Buddha seated on a lotus-petal throne, made in India around the sixth century. It probably passed through the hands of several traders before ending up on the Swedish island of Helgö, more than 5,000 miles from its source.

THE LURE OF FOREIGN TREASURE

Vikings loved strange and alluring objects and traveled great distances to secure them, whether by fair means or foul. As an Arab merchant remarked, Norsemen would go "to any length to get hold of colored beads," but there were many other charms that enticed them abroad. They sought shimmering threads of silver or gold from Byzantium to embroider their tunics, and fine silks from as far away as China to adorn the living and the dead. Not all of the exotic treasures the Vikings craved were obtained at their source. But even when they met merchants from Byzantium, Arabia, or the Orient halfway—at trading centers such as Bulgar, on the Volga River in Russia—the Norsemen still had to undertake long and perilous journeys that rendered the prizes they brought home even more precious.

Vikings sometimes combined in one dazzling setting foreign treasures seized as plunder with items obtained through trade. A necklace crafted by an artisan in Hedeby or in the Swedish trading town of Birka, for example, might include among its ornaments gems or beads stolen from monasteries in the British Isles and silver coins secured through honest exchanges with Arab merchants. It mattered less to the owners how the prize was obtained than how rare or exotic it was. The keepsakes shown here were utterly foreign to Scandinavia—and all the more valuable there as a result. They told of strange worlds that had once been beyond the reach of the Vikings but that now lay within their grasp.

Finely crafted glass objects such as this drinking cup from the Rhineland were among the luxury items imported for aristocratic Vikings.

This ninth-century bronze brazier from Baghdad, resembling a mosque, probably reached Sweden along the Volga River trade route that linked Scandinavia to the Arab world.

There was no reason to lament the dead man's departure, he confidently explained to Ibn Fadlan: "His lord, for love of him, has sent the wind to bring him away in an hour."

Fittingly, when the Viking age in Europe at last came to an end, it went out in a blaze of glory. By the year 1000, the Norsemen were no longer quite the fearsome and irrepressible force they once had been. Christianity was taking hold in Scandinavia, and Vikings were gradually becoming more like other Europeans in their customs and rituals. Two centuries of emigration and political consolidation had eased pressures somewhat within the homeland, and there were not as many young men yearning to go a-viking abroad.

There were still hot battles to be fought, however, and great issues to be decided. As the leaders of the various Viking realms tightened their grip on their subjects and national distinctions grew sharper, fierce rivalries developed between Norse rulers. One of the keenest of those power struggles came to a head in 1066, when Normans led by William the Conqueror crossed the Channel in force and defeated and killed the English king, Harold II Godwinson, who was himself partly of Viking ancestry. Another king died that year vying for the English throne—Harald Hardradi ("the Ruthless") of Norway, who fell to Harold Godwinson's English troops shortly before they in turn succumbed to William's Normans. Of the various contestants in this swirling conflict, Harald of Norway was the one true Viking, unadulterated by French or English influences. In his far-flung exploits, he epitomized the restless Norse spirit, and his death in battle in 1066 marked the end of Viking expansionism in Europe.

Harald Hardradi's saga was too rich for a consummate storyteller like Snorri Sturluson to pass over lightly. Snorri filled 101 chapters of his *Heimskringla* with Harald's ex-

A helmeted warrior with a spear, sword, battle-ax, and sheathed knife at his belt was carved on a stone monument in Viking-held Yorkshire in the 10th century. Vikings were often buried with their weapons.

ploits, following the young prince from Norway to Russia to Byzantium and back to his homeland, where he assumed the throne and ruled with an iron fist before bidding fatally for control of England. In this as in other accounts, Snorri fleshed out the bare bones of the king's career with legends and lore, including lively snippets of verse from court poets who expanded imaginatively on Harald's travails and triumphs. The portrait that emerged was not far from the truth, however, for no ordinary man could have inspired such an array of tributes and embellishments. Harald Hardradi was indeed one of the last great Norse adventurers.

Harald was just 15 when he was forced into exile from his native land after his half brother, Olaf Haraldsson, king of Norway, also known as Saint Olaf, was defeated and killed by Norwegians hostile to his efforts to promote Christianity and wipe out paganism. Harald himself was wounded in the battle that claimed Olaf's life, but he was carried from the field and nursed back to health in a remote farmhouse. Once healed, he escaped to Sweden, avoiding the main trails and hewing to dark forest paths.

After linking up with other exiles in Sweden, Harald and his men decided to offer their services to Yaroslav the Wise, prince of Kiev, who despite his Slavic name claimed descent from the old Swedish rulers of Kiev and confirmed that link by wedding

These menacing iron spears and ax blades, found in the Thames River, were hefted by the Norsemen who invaded England. Although Viking warriors sometimes carried bows and slings, their favorite arms were those used in hand-to-hand fighting.

the daughter of the Swedish king. Harald too had close Swedish ties, and he felt sure of being welcomed by Yaroslav as a comrade and kinsman. So he set out with his company along the well-traveled Rus path, sailing south across the Baltic, then trekking inland by river and trail before reaching the upper Dnieper and descending to Kiev.

Yaroslav wasted no time in putting these keen Vikings to work, enlisting them in a merciless campaign against the Poles and rewarding them for their efforts. (Such was his enduring gratitude that he later gave his daughter Elizabeth to Harald in marriage.) Harald relished the role of mercenary, and after several years with Yaroslav went off with his warriors to play the same part on a grander stage, prowling the Mediterranean in the service of the rulers of Byzantium. One court poet pictured Harald and his men approaching Constantinople for the first time in their longships, with sails billowing above the long, curving prows:

> The great prince saw ahead
> The copper roofs of Byzantium;
> His swan-breasted ships swept
> Towards the tall-towered city.

Fair of hair and beard, Harald had grown strong and tall—taller by a head than the largest of his companions, it was said. One eyebrow perched slightly higher than the other, lending him a rakish look. He charmed the Byzantine empress, Zoë, and those close to her said that she secretly longed to marry him—although she already had a husband and consort, the emperor Michael, and Harald was still pining for that "golden lady in Russia," Elizabeth, who had not yet been granted to him. Zoë's fond regard for Harald ultimately turned sour, but at first he was without fault in the eyes of his imperial patrons, who were thrilled to have him pillaging their enemies and

The Varangian guards, like this well-armed recruit shown in a Byzantine mosaic, served Byzantium's rulers both at home and abroad. Many Vikings went to Constantinople to join the guard.

bringing home the spoils, part of which he claimed as his own. According to Snorri, he rose to become head of the Varangian guard, but he and his men did not confine themselves to guarding the palace. Instead, they ranged abroad, attacking restive Greeks, Sicilians, and others who challenged Byzantine authority and looting their strongholds and sanctuaries.

The Byzantines thought of the Vikings as bloodthirsty barbarians, but Harald Hardradi, like other successful Norse commanders, relied as much on cunning as on brute force. While campaigning with his Varangians in Sicily, Snorri related, Harald used a novel stratagem to overcome one town whose walls were too strong to be broken down—he enlisted the help of birds that nested under the eaves of the houses there. Every day, Snorri explained, the birds flew out into the surrounding countryside in search of

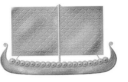

tise his condition to his foes in town but simply remained out of sight and let their spies take credit for discovering his plight. When a mournful delegation of Varangians sought a parley with the townspeople a short time later and announced that Harald had died, the Sicilians were neither surprised nor suspicious. They should have smelled trouble when the Vikings asked to bury Harald inside their walls, but greed got the better of them. Among the town leaders were churchmen who were eager to claim the remains of Harald—a Christian in name if not in deed—in hopes of garnering the rich gifts that flowed to holy places sheltering the bones of wealthy and powerful men, however ill-gotten their gains.

So eager were the townspeople to exploit Harald's demise that they made a ceremony of it, welcoming his coffin as if it held the body of a saint.

"With all her might she could not have prevented him from marrying the girl."

food, and the observant Harald had his men capture a number of them and tie to their backs shavings of fir, coated with a combustible mixture of wax and sulfur. His men then set the shavings alight and released the birds, which flew straight back to their nests in town and kindled fires on the thatched roofs that spread to surrounding buildings. The terrified inhabitants forced open the town gates and rushed out into the waiting arms of Harald and company, who claimed the place without a fight.

Another fortified town in Sicily proved an even more formidable target and seemed impervious to any tactic or trick. But Harald outdid himself—and his enemies. After laying siege to the stronghold for a while, he took to his bunk and remained there, by all appearances gravely ill. Shrewdly, he did not adver-

"All the clergy donned their robes and came out of the town in a splendid procession, bearing shrines and other holy relics," Snorri related. The Varangians met them in a "magnificent cortege, carrying the coffin on high under a canopy of precious cloth and many banners." As the pallbearers reached the threshold of town, however, they set the coffin down between the yawning gates to keep them open and unsheathed their swords amid the blast of trumpets, sounding the call to arms. Monks and priests who moments before had been eagerly awaiting Viking gifts ran in terror from their presumed benefactors. Harald's men rampaged through the city, slaying cleric and layman alike and looting the holy places whose guardians had hoped to profit by the passing of Harald, now miraculously resurrected.

THE BATTLE FOR THE THRONE

The Norman conquest of England in the year 1066, celebrated in these scenes from the Bayeux tapestry, capped an epic struggle involving three rulers with varying degrees of Viking ancestry. Although William the Conqueror and his Normans were of Norse heritage and adorned their ships with dragon prows *(below)*, they were Frenchmen above all. William's English adversary, Harold Godwinson, was related through his Scandinavian mother to King Canute—a Dane who had seized the English throne in 1016—and thus was somewhat closer than William to the Viking tradition. The third contestant, King Harald Hardradi of Norway, was a full-blooded Norseman who needed little excuse to wage war.

William, perhaps more concerned than the others with justifying his aggression, cited Harold Godwinson's promise to support him as successor to Edward the Confessor, king of England, who died without an heir in January of 1066. In fact, that pledge had been extracted from Harold under duress after he was shipwrecked off the coast of Normandy and ended up in William's custody. The real question was not who deserved the throne but who had the strength to take it. Harold's grasp appeared less than firm, and both William and Harald Hardradi saw a chance to wrest the prize away from him.

As luck would have it, ill winds kept

Norman servants straining like beasts of burden pull a cart loaded with a huge wine barrel, helmets, and lances to ships bound for England. Behind them, men use spears to carry the cumbersome chain mail tunics worn in battle by William's troops.

Norman soldiers torch an English estate as the distraught mistress of the house leads her son away from the flames.

Their sails billowing in the long-awaited wind, the impatient Normans cross the English Channel along with their horses and supplies.

William's fleet penned up in port while Harald Hardradi forged ahead and lost his army and his life at Stamford Bridge, a battle that cost the victorious English forces dearly as well. When at last the winds turned favorable, one chronicle related, William's men "raised their hands and voices in thanks to heaven." They should have given thanks for the circumstances that delayed them. By the time they reached England in their ships—packed from bow to stern with men, horses, supplies, and arms— one of William's rivals had been destroyed and the other weakened.

William was not just fortunate, he was also a gifted commander who had amassed a formidable army of about 7,000 men, including hundreds of archers and a sizable cavalry contingent. England's King Harold faced him with a force of about the same size, but they were weary and mostly on foot. Eager to provoke them into immediate confrontation, William told his men to lay waste the English countryside.

The two forces met on a hilltop near the town of Hastings. Harold's men fought gamely, but William's cavalry overcame them. By one account, Harold was felled by a Norman horseman and "stripped of all badges of honour," so that he could be identified "only by certain marks on his body." Proceeding to London in triumph, William the Conqueror was crowned king of England on Christmas Day, 1066.

William rallies his troops, saying, "Now is the time for you to show your strength. There is no road for retreat."

King Harold's housecarls—his select guards—try valiantly to withstand the onslaught of Norman cavalrymen spurred on by William's exhortations. To protect themselves, Harold's men formed a so-called shield wall, standing so close together that even some of those who have been slain remain upright.

Harold is cut down by a Norman knight, effectively ending the Battle of Hastings.

If Harald Hardradi was half as crafty as these tales suggest, he must have given his opponents grief and all but his firmest friends cause for unrest. Even his imperial patrons, who did well by his skulduggery, came to resent and distrust him. After many rewarding campaigns, he returned to Constantinople and resigned his command, having learned that the Norwegian ruler who had supplanted his half brother, Olaf, had been deposed and that his nephew, Magnus Olafsson, was now king. His own claim to power was stronger than his nephew's, he felt, and he was eager to return to Norway and assert it. But Empress Zoë was unwilling to let Harald slip away. She accused him of withholding from the imperial couple their full share of the plunder and had him imprisoned. Perhaps she still longed for him and wanted to keep him close, but her passion went unrequited. The only woman who came close to rivaling the distant Elizabeth in Harald's affections was Zoë's alluring niece, Maria, and the empress was not about to let Harald have her.

No prison could hold Harald for long. With help from confederates, he escaped from the dungeon, roused his Varangians, and assailed the emperor and put out his eyes. Then, to add insult to injury, he abducted Maria and carried her off in his longship. The great iron chains at the mouth of the Bosporus blocked his exit, Snorri attested, but the ever-resourceful Harald moved his gear sternward to elevate the prow and slipped up and over the chains with a mighty assist from his oarsmen. Once safely free of Zoë's grasp, he put Maria ashore and bade her return to Constantinople and remind the empress how little power she had over him, "for with all her might she could not have prevented him from marrying the girl."

In truth, Maria was dispensable. On his way back to Norway, Harald stopped off in Russia and renewed his suit for the hand of Elizabeth. Yaroslav could see by all the treasure Harald had accumulated that he was worthy of a princess, and he sanctioned the match. As one poet put it:

The warlike king of Norway
Won the match of his desire,
He gained a king's daughter
And a hoard of gold as well.

Harald was not quite king yet, but he was close enough to taste it. After sailing to Sweden, he forged a temporary alliance with Elizabeth's cousin, Svein Ulfsson (who harbored royal ambitions of his own), assembled a formidable war fleet, and made things so hot for King Magnus that the leader finally agreed to share power with his bothersome kinsman. When Magnus died in 1047, Harald became sole ruler, but he still faced stiff challenges to his authority. As always, there were powerful men in Norway who resented the king's claim to preeminence and defied him. Harald duped and destroyed such foes without scruple, in one case hacking to death a troublesome chieftain whom he had invited to court to talk peace. A poem attributed to Harald suggested that he reveled in his ruthless reputation:

Now I have caused the deaths
Of thirteen of my enemies;
I kill without compunction,
And remember all my killings.
Treason must be scotched
By fair means or foul.

The greatest challenges Harald met with during his reign came from abroad, however. By this time, conquests, compacts, and marriage alliances had greatly complicated relations between the ruling families of Norway, Denmark, Sweden, England, and Normandy, providing Harald and other ambitious rulers with pretexts for usurping power overseas. The kings of Norway and Denmark, for example, had long claimed a right to each other's domain, and Harald carried on in that bloody tradition, battling furiously with his in-law and former ally, Svein Ulfsson, who had taken charge in Denmark and coveted Norway as well. Harald defeated Svein's forces in a great sea battle in 1062, but Svein himself escaped, and two years later the rival monarchs reached a grudging pact that confirmed "the ancient boundaries between the two countries," in Snorri's words.

Neither Harald nor his warriors laid down their weapons for long. As one old Viking chieftain put it, King Harald "went to war for fame and power," and he could never get enough of either. His last great chance came in January of 1066, when Edward the Confessor, king of England, died and was succeeded by Harold Godwinson, whose claim to the throne was contested by William of Normandy. Egged on by Harold's resentful brother, Tostig, Harald Hardradi decided to bid for power in England as well. Earlier in the century, Danes had seized and occupied the English throne for a time, and Harald hoped to emulate them.

But it was not to be. Harald and his warriors were out of their element in England, and they were taken by surprise at Stamford Bridge. They had little room to maneuver. All they could do was stand and fall. They took a steep toll of Harold Godwinson's forces in the process and thus contributed indirectly to the Norman conquest at Hastings less than a month later. But the Battle of Stamford Bridge was a crushing defeat both for Harald Hardradi—who lost his life along with thousands of his followers—and for the Viking ambitions he personified. The age of the Normans might be dawning, but here in England and on the Continent, at least, the days of the Norsemen were done. No longer would their longships, as graceful as swans and as dreadful as dragons, be the wonder and terror of Europe.

BIRTH OF THE VIKING SHIP

Their lands awash in rivers and lakes, edged by fjords *(below),* and bounded by the sea, the Scandinavians became skilled boatbuilders and handlers, crafting oar-propelled boats to fish local waters and to travel to nearby settlements. The restless Norse of the eighth century, however, wanted to travel farther. To do so, they needed crafts powerful enough for extended voyages. From that need was born the longship—proudly reproduced by the Scandinavians on objects like this stylized 13th-century city seal *(inset).* The longship loosed the Norse on the world and launched the Viking era.

CRAFTING A DRAGON

To a 2,000-year legacy of light and flexible vessels, Viking shipbuilders added a sail for speed and power, a sturdy mast, and a long keel for extra stability in the sea, but they retained a draft shallow enough to navigate rivers. These Viking vessels with double-ended hulls and pronounced keels were known as longships. The largest of them were called *drekar*, or dragon ships, and were built to carry the Norse on raids and into battle. But not all of the crafts were longships. The *knorr*, a wider craft with a central, open cargo hold, transported colonists and traders alike to their destinations. Unlike the longship, which sported a continuous row of oars for greater maneuverability, the knorr relied mainly on its sail, using oars only at stem and stern.

To build their vessels, master shipwrights commanded a platoon of workers, most with their own areas of expertise. Selecting the right trees, for instance, was crucial. Woodsmen sought out tall, straight oaks for long keels and planking and other trees with natural bends and twists for curved pieces. At the end of the process, skilled artisans decorated the ships with their carvings, which might take the form of beautiful interlocking designs or a menacing dragon head.

Intricate carvings and a coiled snake decorate the prow of this ninth-century Viking ship from Oseberg, Norway. As with most Scandinavian vessels, the ship's planks are nailed securely together in a clinker-built, or overlapping, pattern.

Ax raised, a man prepares to fell a tree, while nearby another straddles a rough plank supported in a tree cleft and trims it with a T-shaped ax *(right)*. Below, two builders work on a ship with an auger and a hand ax. These vignettes from the Bayeux tapestry are thought to portray the actual stages of Viking-style shipbuilding.

Diamond-patterned sail unfurled overhead, a Norse ship skims over the water in a Gotland picture stone carved around AD 700. While the helmsman steers the ship with a large side rudder, others control the sail with an intricate network of rigging.

On the 13th-century carving above, a fleet of Viking ships feature both figure-heads and weather vanes like the 11th-century gilded-bronze vane at right. Not merely decorative, a dragon head served to intimidate the enemy, while the weather vane helped the helmsman maintain the best sailing angle.

SETTING SAIL

The Viking ship's sail, a large rectangular sheet of woven wool, provided great power, but wild winds or a soaking from a rainstorm made it difficult to maneuver. The Norwegian king Eystein lost his life when an uncontrolled yard on the ship next to his swung out and knocked him into the ocean. Still, Viking mariners took great pride in their sails, which often sported red stripes or diamond designs. One chieftain refused to continue his journey until a favorable wind arrived to billow out his sail so he could display it boldly as he sailed along a foreign coast.

Whenever possible, most Norse ships hugged the coast-line, not to show off their sails but to use familiar landmarks for guides. Navigation at sea was more complicated. Though Vikings probably had some crude instruments, they relied heavily on sun and star positions, wind direction, wave patterns, water color and temperature, and the presence of certain birds and sea mammals to ascertain their position. They were intrepid explorers, who sometimes simply set out across the ocean into the unknown, relying on their sea skills to bring them safely home.

TOSSED AMID THE WAVES

The open deck of the ship afforded little protection from the elements. Although the men wrapped themselves in fur and oiled skins, wind, rain, and the constant spray of water kept many Viking sailors cold and wet. Nightfall usually offered a welcome respite. When near land, the Vikings went ashore to cook hot meals and sleep in tents. On long sea voyages, however, the travelers subsisted on a diet of dried and salted fish or meat, and they huddled in two-man animal-skin sleeping bags laid out on the deck.

For all the Scandinavians' seagoing expertise, they and their vessels often succumbed to the harsh waters in which they sailed. Many died from the damp and cold while others drowned in shipwrecks. But the Vikings had been born to go to sea. Though they remained home during the long winter months, cleaning and repairing their ships, in April they eagerly set forth once again. One early medieval chronicler made an observation that, though written about the Danes, surely applied to all who went a-viking: They "live in the sea."

The deck of a ninth-century ship from Gokstad, Norway, viewed from near the helmsman's position, holds a ridged gangplank *(below, right)* and several oars *(below, left)*. Behind the center mast jut the arms of a T-shaped trestle, one of a row upon which the sail may have been stored.

A bailer *(left)*, thrust into the hull through gaps in the deck, allowed the Vikings to scoop seawater out of the ship. In bad weather, the sagas say, almost as many sailors might be bailing as rowing.

In this modern drawing, Norse settlers fight to keep their ship afloat during a sudden storm as the sail snaps wildly overhead and water rushes in. The helmsman struggles for control while others bail furiously.

"We sailed our ships

to any shore

that offered the best

hope of booty;

we feared

no fellow on earth,

we were fit, we fought

in the battle-fleet."

—Saga of Arrow-Odd

Dragon head rearing
against the reddish gold sky
of a Scandinavian sunset, a
modern Danish replica of a
Viking longship proudly
sails the northern waters.

CHAPTER THREE

TO ICELAND AND BEYOND

The foggy, wind-swept shores of the Faeroe Islands harbored Viking settlers and served as steppingstones for Norse expansion westward to Iceland in the ninth century. Populated by Scandinavians, the Faeroes and Iceland long preserved their Viking roots.

tanding at the prow of their hardy little vessel, the foster brothers Ingolf and Leif marveled at the great island that lay ahead. They and their crew had voyaged some 700 miles across the gale-riven North Atlantic. Now at last they were nearing their destination. As a brisk wind ballooned their square sail they approached the east coast of the island, creased with glacial fjords reminiscent of their native Norway. The hillsides were green with tall grass and dotted with scrub birch and juniper. Yet beyond those welcoming slopes loomed angry volcanic peaks, wreathed in snow but still simmering within.

Amid this volatile landscape of fire and ice, the newcomers found life in abundance. Entering one of the fjords, they saw seals darting through the clear waters in pursuit of salmon and cod. Overhead, hosts of seabirds circled raucously, while others nested on nearby cliffs. Encouraged, the men dropped anchor and went ashore. No one was there to greet them, for aside from a few Irish monks who had made this desolate place their hermitage, the island was uninhabited. Perhaps the Norwegians heard distant volcanic rumblings and felt the earth tremble, as if trying to shake them off, but they held fast.

The leaders of this pioneering party, Ingolf Arnarson and Leif

Hrodmarsson, had set out with little more to guide them than vague and contradictory reports. A decade or so earlier, around the year 860, a Norwegian called Naddod and a Swede named Gardar had come upon this island separately when their ships were blown off course. A few years after their chance discovery, another venturesome Norwegian, known as Raven Floki for the birds he carried on board to release in search of land, spent a bitter winter here with his family and followers and dubbed the place Iceland. He left the next summer, thoroughly discouraged. Nonetheless, one of his men touted Iceland as a land of plenty, where "butter dripped from every blade of grass." He may have been imagining cows grazing on the green hillsides and yielding milk and butter. In any case, his claims offered hope to the likes of Ingolf and Leif. They were searching for refuge, having killed two sons of a chieftain after one of them flirted with Helga, Ingolf's sister and Leif's future wife. Forced to surrender their estates to appease the chieftain, they set out to recoup their fortunes in Iceland.

Unlike Raven Floki, Ingolf and Leif made thorough preparations before bringing their families to Iceland. As related in an Icelandic chronicle called *The Book of Settlements,* their first journey was merely a reconnaissance, designed to see if the land was indeed livable. They built a shelter and wintered in Iceland with their crew, discovering to their satisfaction that although the wind howled and snow fell, there were mild spells, thanks to the moderating effect of warm ocean currents. As spring advanced and the hillsides and meadows took on a fresh coat of green,

prospects for settlement seemed as bright as the northern lights that shimmered in the night sky.

Their minds made up, the foster brothers returned to Norway, where Ingolf readied their households for the move while Leif sailed off to plunder in Ireland for bounty that might enable them to make a prosperous start in their new country. Among the prizes Leif seized was a great sword that he used on his raids for treasure, earning him the name Hjorleif, or Sword-Leif. Along the way he captured and enslaved 10 Irishmen. As it turned out, those slaves, like the rest of his plunder, would bring him little but grief.

After Hjorleif returned to Norway, the foster brothers—joined by their wives, family members, slaves, and a group of neighboring freemen—put to sea in two ships. Ingolf's boat was crowded with household goods and cattle, while Hjorleif's was packed with the Irish booty. Hjorleif, trusting to his own devices,

A sturdy Viking merchant ship weathers rough seas in this illustration from an Icelandic lawbook. Known as knorrs, such vessels were shorter and bulkier than the sleek, dragon-headed longships used for warfare and rode deeper in the water, making them more stable in swells. They proved ideal both for transporting settlers and livestock and for carrying the trade goods needed to sustain Iceland and other isolated Viking colonies.

offered no gifts to the gods before he departed. The pious Ingolf, by contrast, made sacrifices to Thor and stashed aboard his ship the sacred pillars of the high seat he occupied in his hall, carved with images of the gods.

As the ships neared the southeast coast of Iceland, Ingolf tossed his pillars overboard, vowing to settle wherever the gods brought them to shore. Then the two parties went their separate ways. Ingolf landed and dutifully went in search of the pillars, while Hjorleif let the wind carry him westward. He and his thirsty crew ran out of drinking water but were saved by a heavy rain, which they caught in the ship's sail. Finally, Hjorleif came ashore near Iceland's southern tip, far from Ingolf's landing place. He and his men set themselves up there in style, it was said, building two great halls, each more than 100 feet long, which sheltered them through the winter.

Come spring, Hjorleif was ready to till the ground, but amid all the glittering treasure he had carried to Iceland, he had with him only one ox. Not to be deterred, he yoked his Irish slaves to the plow alongside the ox. They were proud men and hated being treated like beasts. Conspiring against their master, they killed the ox and blamed its death on a marauding bear, in hopes of tricking Hjorleif into chasing after the animal at his own peril. As a newcomer, he could hardly know that Iceland harbored no such predators, other than the stray polar bears that appeared now and then on ice floes off the north coast.

Hjorleif and his followers set out to find the phantom, separating from one another to cover more ground. Soon the hunters became the hunted. Still smarting from their ill treatment, the slaves tracked down and murdered each man in turn, then fled to a small island off the coast, taking with them their late master's wife, Helga, and the other women of the party.

Their crime did not go undetected. Some time later, mem-

bers of Ingolf's party, still searching for the elusive pillars, came upon his brother's body and guessed the truth. "This was a sorry end for a brave man," he lamented, "that slaves should be the death of him." It seemed to Ingolf that his foster brother had been punished for his impiety. Such was the fate, he concluded, of those "not prepared to offer up sacrifice." After burying the victims, Ingolf tracked the murderers down, catching them by surprise while they were feasting and slaughtering several on the spot. The others tumbled off the edge of a cliff in terror and fell to their deaths. Ingolf rescued the women seized by the slaves and offered them refuge among his party, then resumed his quest.

At length, two of Ingolf's slaves, named Vifil and Karli, found the sacred pillars along an inlet far to the west, and their master fulfilled his pledge by settling there with his band. The site hardly seemed a gift from the gods. Volcanic craters dominated a bleak lava plain. At times a thick fog rolled in from the bay to mingle with the vapors from geysers and hot sulfur springs. Ingolf named the place Reykjavik, or Smoky Bay, and it would later become the capital of Iceland.

Not everyone was pleased with Ingolf for accepting this as their ordained home. "We traveled past good country to bad purpose," complained the slave Karli, who soon ran off with a slave woman. Others abided by their leader's decision, however, and remained with him. Among those who kept faith with Ingolf was the slave Vifil, who was rewarded by his master with freedom and who established his own homestead. Vifil "lived many a long day," the chronicle related, and he was honored and respected as a "trusty man."

From the persistence and devotion of such pioneers as Ingolf and Vifil emerged a tight-knit colony with a profound respect for law and tradition. But Icelandic society was also imbued with the defiant spirit of men like Karli and the murdered Hjorleif, who bridled at restraint and pursued their own reckless paths. Here as elsewhere in the Viking world, such unruliness had mixed con-

Volcanic debris darkens a glacier in southeast Iceland. The Vikings who ventured to this so-called Land of Fire and Ice also encountered more inviting prospects, including sheltered fjords and green valleys that supported settlements.

sequences, sowing discord in Iceland but inspiring bold new ventures that carried Norse outlaws and adventurers westward to Greenland and the shores of the New World.

Over the next 60 years many Vikings followed Ingolf's example and crossed the northern sea to Iceland, bringing its population to nearly 20,000. Some were fleeing the tyranny of Harald Fairhair, who was tightening his grip on Norway. Most were simply looking for land and livelihood at a time when the Viking population was outgrowing the resources of sparse areas such as Norway's southwestern coast. A few emigrants made the journey from other parts of Scandinavia and mingled with the Norwegian majority in Iceland, lured by the promise of a fresh start in a new country.

For all its attractions, Iceland proved to be neither a place of limitless bounty nor a refuge from the problems of the old world. Indeed, some of the tensions that were eased in the homeland by emigration and foreign conquest persisted and deepened in Iceland, which eventually ran short of land for settlers and their burgeoning families and offered no convenient outlet for restless young Vikings and their combative energies. Some made the long and uncertain journey back to Europe and went a-viking there, and a few bold spirits ultimately sailed off in search of uncharted territory. Most settlers who felt hemmed in, however, had little choice but to vent their frustrations on neighbors, engaging in feuds as stubborn and vicious as any that flared up back in the homeland.

There was plenty for people to feud over, aside from issues of land or livestock. Fearful of tyranny, Icelanders acknowledged no king, but the absence of higher authority left chieftains free to flex their muscles and carry out bloody vendettas against rival lords and their followers. The time-honored Viking custom of meeting in public assemblies to pronounce laws and resolve disputes flourished as never before in Iceland, but enforcement was left to the aggrieved parties, and their rough justice often provoked further violence. Even

Scenes from an Icelandic law-book portray the dividing of a beached whale—to be shared by the finder with the owner of the land where the whale washed ashore—and the hanging of a sheep rustler, whose offense was considered to be worse than murder.

the eventual introduction of Christianity and its gospel of peace stirred up trouble, as converts and those faithful to the old Norse gods vied for authority.

Little of this was evident in the early decades of settlement, when good land was plentiful and a malcontent like Ingolf's slave Karli could simply run off and start anew elsewhere. According to one saga, Iceland remained a place of ample opportunity at the dawn of the 10th century, when Aud the Deep-Minded—the resourceful Norwegian noblewoman who had lost her husband in Ireland and her son in Scotland before setting out across the North Atlantic with what remained of her family and fortune—reached the budding colony to join her two brothers, who had immigrated earlier. No stranger to adversity, she met with a fresh setback off the coast of Iceland when her ship struck a reef and sank, but she made it safely to shore with her sizable retinue, including family members, slaves, and 20 retainers who were free but faithful to her. All of them descended in some disarray on her brother Helgi, who dutifully welcomed his sister but refused to house more than nine of her companions.

Helgi may simply have lacked the wherewithal to host so many visitors. But the fiery Aud denounced him as "mean-spirited" and stalked out with her entire entourage to seek the hospitality of her other brother, Bjorn. He "knew his sister's nature," related the saga, and gave her no reason to fault his generosity. As it turned out, he did not have to support the visitors for long. Aud had not come to Iceland to be dependent on anyone. She soon took possession of "as much land as she pleased," parceling out lots to her followers, including the slaves she freed, thereby keeping them beholden to her and enhancing her position as head of an important household.

In the end, Aud died splendidly, just as she had lived. After betrothing her grandson to a woman of good family, she hosted an elegant feast to celebrate his marriage and announced to the guests that she was bestowing on the bridegroom her house and land. She urged the revelers to make free with the ale and enjoy themselves to the full,

then graciously took her leave. They found her dead the next morning in bed, sitting bolt upright. As befitted a noble Viking, she was buried on a ship with a portion of her treasure—more than enough, presumably, to carry her to the next world in comfort on this her last great voyage.

Aud may have acquired as much land as she wished, but not all who immigrated when she did or in later years were so fortunate. Iceland was a big place, larger than Ireland, but much of it was uninhabitable. Roughly three quarters of its surface was covered by peat bogs, glaciers, moraines, volcanoes, and lava beds—fine places for trolls and giants, perhaps, but of little use to mortals. The early settlers claimed much of the best land, leaving the latecomers to fight for their share.

So fierce were the squabbles over land, according to one chronicle, that in the early 900s Icelanders swallowed their pride and asked Norway's much-maligned ruler, Harald Fairhair, to mediate a settlement. The agreement he worked out limited each man to as much territory as he could encompass in a single day while carrying a flaming torch. A woman could stake out only as much land as she could walk around in a day while leading a two-year-old heifer.

Soon there was nothing left to be claimed that was worth having. By 930 the era of settlement had come to an end. It was not just land that was scarce. The forests of scrub birch and evergreens that looked so inviting to the pioneers were soon depleted, and Icelanders had to warm their hearths by burning driftwood or sheep dung. From the beginning Iceland was devoid of tall, sturdy hardwoods such as oak or elm, ideal for building houses and boats. Some early settlers found enough timber of other kinds to construct wooden houses. Others built homes of turf and stone, up to 100 feet long, with earthen walls several feet thick, which provided ample insulation, and sod-covered roofs with the grass still attached and growing. To build boats, however, Icelanders had no alternative but to purchase wood from abroad. They also imported flour and malt, since most of their land was used for grazing and they did not grow enough grain to meet their own needs. Ships from Norway also brought in iron, linen, wax, tin and soapstone vessels, weapons, jewelry, and other luxuries and necessities, all of which cost Icelanders dearly.

In time the settlers ran out of silver to pay for the imports and instead offered visiting merchants sheepskins, livestock, falcons, sulfur, dairy products, and a rough woolen fabric they called *vadmál*. Measured out in ells—lengths equivalent to a given value in silver—this popular homespun cloth became the local medium of exchange. To keep foreign merchants from playing off one eager buyer against another, three Icelandic men were appointed to set the prices for goods as each ship landed.

That was just one of the ways in which Icelanders tried to bring order to their competitive and contentious world. As much as the settlers dreaded tyranny, they were equally wary of lawlessness. As one landowner put it, they wanted to be "free of kings and criminals." Order was preserved locally by chieftains, some of whom also

Lacking timber, Icelanders built longhouses like this reconstruction, framed of turf atop a stone foundation. One side chamber housed the dairy, and the other may have served as a lavatory. The occupants passed the winters inside, saving their wood for articles like the lidded vessel at right, which served as a bowl or cup.

used the title of *godi,* or priest, and held court near shrines they maintained, thus investing their rulings with divine authority.

Those local courts were powerless to resolve disputes that crossed lines and pitted one chieftain and his followers against a rival band. To handle such larger quarrels, the Icelanders expanded on the Viking tradition of meeting in communal councils, called *things,* and instituted four regional councils, known as *quarter things.* There was also a paramount assembly of all the country's landowners, known as the Althing, which convened for two weeks each summer at Thingvellir, near Reykjavik, to settle matters that no other body could resolve.

By virtue of this remarkable assembly—a kind of parliament—Iceland constituted a republic, or free state, one without parallel in Scandinavia or any of the

Icelanders at all levels of society were torn between respect for law and a longing for vengeance that sometimes ran contrary to the pronouncements of the lawspeaker or the rulings of councils. Like the volcanoes that brooded over their landscape, people could nurse grudges quietly for years and then suddenly erupt. When blood was shed, the law called for an ascending scale of fines—usually assessed in silver but sometimes in cattle or homespun—ranging from payment to the aggrieved family of a modest sum for the killing of a slave to a hefty fine for the slaughter of a prominent landholder. Wrongdoers whose violent ways posed an exceptional threat to their neighbors were outlawed, either for three years or, in the worst cases, for life. These bloodless penalties were meant to avert further feuding, for even the

> *"You will find it hard to compensate for all the damage Hallgerd will cause."*

other European lands visited by the Vikings. The republic's only paid official was the lawspeaker, a powerful chieftain in his own right, who was elected by his peers to serve for three years and recited the laws of the land, based on Scandinavian precedents but adapted to suit circumstances in Iceland. The lawspeaker exercised only moral authority and had no troops with which to punish lawbreakers. Power remained in the hands of the local chieftains, each of whom commanded the allegiance of the farmers within his district. Although chieftains often tried to resolve disputes through mediation or lawful assemblies, they were prepared to impose their will with the help of their armed followers.

Nor were chieftains the only ones who stirred up trouble.

killing of a confessed murderer invited retribution. On the other hand, fining the wrongdoer or exiling him did not always satisfy the victim's kin, and their unsanctioned acts of violence kept vendettas alive.

The conflict between the respect for law and the lust for vengeance was vividly chronicled in *Njal's Saga,* an anonymous Icelandic account relating tragic events there in the late 10th and early 11th centuries. The saga's principal figure, a prudent and judicious man named Njal, labored heroically to keep peace with his fair-minded but more impulsive friend Gunnar despite a murderous feud nurtured by their wives and abetted by others in the two households. Against great odds, the two men preserved

their friendship, but they ultimately became victims of an ever-expanding vendetta that pitted some of Iceland's leading families against one another.

Ironically, the seeds of discord were sown at the Althing, the annual meeting intended to resolve differences. More than just an assembly, the Althing was a great festive gathering. Women and youngsters sometimes joined their menfolk for the occasion. Leading families occupied booths, or lodges, on the assembly grounds, and others camped in the vicinity. At night they sat by the fire, trading tales and reciting poems. Romances blossomed in the lingering twilight, and marriages were arranged.

Among those who found a wife there one summer was the handsome Gunnar, a noble young man of unfailing grace and courage who had traveled to Scandinavia and been hosted by royalty and was now ready to settle down on his estate in Iceland and start a family. Graced with "keen blue eyes, red cheeks, and a fine head of thick flaxen hair," he strolled through the grounds wearing splendid robes given to him by a Danish king and a golden armlet from one of Norway's leading lords.

No man at the Althing could compare with him, it was said, but at least one woman seemed a match for him in appearance and bearing. Her name was Hallgerd, and she was garbed in a "red, richly-decorated tunic under a scarlet cloak trimmed all the way down with lace." Her hair was so long and thick that "she could hide herself in it." While other women waited demurely to be approached by the desirable Gunnar, Hallgerd greeted him boldly and asked him to tell her about his travels. Gunnar liked nothing better, and he soon found himself exchanging confidences with a woman he barely knew. He was delighted to learn that she was unmarried and had no suitors.

"Do you think no one good enough for you?" he teased.

"Not at all," she responded. "But I may be a little particular about husbands."

That was putting it mildly. As Gunnar soon discovered, she had been married twice, and both of her husbands had been killed after quarreling with the overparticular Hallgerd and slapping her—injuries promptly avenged by her violently possessive foster father. Gunnar would not have to compete with the foster father, who had recently met with the death he deserved. But Hallgerd alone was challenge enough for any man. She claimed descent on her father's side from Sigurd the Dragon-Killer, and indeed, she resembled that legendary figure in her determination and cunning. Had she been born a boy, she might well have been grudgingly admired by her fellow Vikings for the way she avenged perceived slights and prosecuted feuds. But as a woman, she was reduced to the sorry role of prodding others to fulfill her violent designs. Njal warned his friend Gunnar that she would be "nothing but trouble," but Gunnar was spellbound. Perhaps it was not only her beauty that charmed him but something fierce and defiant in her that aroused his combative instincts.

MANUSCRIPTS FOR THE MASSES

Icelanders, whose sagas were among the great works of medieval literature, preserved their writings in sturdy bindings like that enclosing the copy of *Njal's Saga* below. Texts were inscribed on vellum of tanned sheepskin or calfskin, using quill pens dipped in bearberry ink.

Some Icelandic manuscripts, like the 13th-century edition of the law code at right, contained illustrations or decorative flourishes, but they were not as richly illuminated as works penned in Europe for palaces or cloisters. Icelandic books were copied in relatively large numbers so that they could be read by all.

The peace-loving Njal, by contrast, encouraged Gunnar never to lash out in anger without pondering the bitter consequences. As the saga related, Njal was a "gentle man of great integrity; he remembered the past and discerned the future." Older and wiser than Gunnar, he knew the law as well as any man in Iceland and lived by its principles of compromise and conciliation. He was fully prepared to tolerate insults from Gunnar's new bride in order to keep the peace. Unfortunately, Njal's wife of many years, Bergthora, was not so forbearing. In the words of the saga, she was "an exceptional and courageous woman, but a little harsh-natured." In truth, many Vikings were courageous but a little harsh natured, and few could fault Njal's wife for the spirited way in which she responded to Hallgerd's provocations.

The showdown came not long after Gunnar's wedding, when he and Hallgerd attended a feast at Njal's house. In the halls of wealthy Vikings, much as in the courts of Scandinavian kings, the status of those present was signaled by how close they sat to the host. As Gunnar's wife, Hallgerd was afforded a place of honor, close to Njal's high seat. But when Njal's daughter-in-law arrived belatedly, Bergthora asked Hallgerd to move down to make room for the newcomer. "I'm not moving down for anyone, like some outcast hag," responded Hallgerd. Bergthora insisted, pointing out to her unruly guest that the mistress of the house had absolute authority in such matters. After reluctantly yielding, Hallgerd goaded her hostess with a tactless reference to the fact that Njal was beardless—no small deficiency in a land where

THE POWER OF POETRY

Late one summer in the 10th century, a shrewd and combative Icelander named Egill Skallagrimsson sailed for England, steering well clear of Norway, where he had earned the hatred of King Erik Blood-axe in earlier years. Egill soon had reason to regret the journey. First his ship foundered off the coast of northern England, then, after he stumbled ashore, he fell into the hands of his old enemy, Erik Bloodaxe, who had been driven from Norway by his brother and now held court in Viking-held York as king of Northumbria.

Erik sentenced Egill to death and gave him one night to prepare himself. No weapon could save Egill, but he thought that words might. Aside from being a ruthless warrior, he was also a gifted poet who composed skaldic verse, filled with puzzling metaphors called kennings and used to praise heroes and their feats. As the dark hours of night slipped away, Egill labored to compose such a praise poem in honor of Erik and thus win a reprieve.

When he appeared before the king the next morning for execution, Egill appealed to Erik in verse:

> A song in praise
> of the prince I raise,
> and him now pray
> to hear my lay . . .

Erik was intrigued and allowed Egill to continue. What followed was a long and convoluted tribute to the king's prowess in battle. Those unfamiliar with skaldic verse and its kennings would have been baffled by the poem, but Erik was knowledgeable enough to interpret such verses and vain enough to be flattered by them:

> Did the shower-of-darts
> strike shield-ramparts
> of the prince's array
> as he plunged in the fray;
> when on the sands
> of surf-beaten strands,
> brimming with blood,
> the battle stood. . . .
>
> Slammed halberds dire
> 'gainst helmet-fire,
> bit wingèd arrow
> into warriors' marrow;
> by steel ice-cold
> struck, I am told,
> fell Odin's-trees
> in weapon-breeze.

Egill concluded by praising Erik's generosity, and his words seemed to work like a charm. "You can have your head as a present," the king told him. Erik credited the reprieve to one of his counselors, who argued for mercy, but the poem obviously helped Egill escape death, and it was known

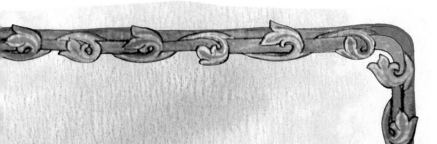

thereafter as his "Head Ransom."

The poem and the incident that inspired it were recorded 300 years later in *Egil's Saga* by Snorri Sturluson, a descendant of Egill Skallagrimsson. Snorri also wrote a treatise on Norse poetry in which he interpreted the old kennings used by Egill and his fellow skalds. The term "helmet-fire," for instance, was a kenning for sword, inspired by the image of a sword striking a metal helmet and kicking up sparks. The phrase "Odin's-trees in weapon-breeze" meant men in battle, because Viking warriors were devoted to the god Odin and stood or fell by his power.

Odin's name was often invoked by poets, for legend has it he stole the sacred mead of poetry—guarded by giants and created by dwarfs from the blood of a sage—and shared its mysteries with the people who worshiped him. Like other fabled exploits, Odin's feat inspired a kenning: Vikings referred to poetry as the "drink of the dwarfs."

all men who could grow beards did so to proclaim their virility. "That's true," Bergthora shot back, and yet she never faulted Njal for it, whereas Hallgerd's first husband had been handsomely bearded, and "that didn't stop you from having him killed."

At that, Hallgerd turned to Gunnar. Some called him the "bravest man in Iceland," she said scathingly, but what good was that to her if he failed to avenge such insults?

Furious at his wife, Gunnar insisted that they leave at once and suggested that Hallgerd confine her venom henceforth to her own household. He had kind words for Njal, but the damage had been done. In such proud circles, insults could be lethal, and neither woman would forget or forgive the cutting words exchanged across the table.

Significantly, their feud turned violent while Njal and Gunnar were away at the next Althing, leaving the wives to pursue their own brand of justice. Viking women often controlled the household, supervising slaves and hiring servants as needed. Such retainers were naturally beholden to the mistress of the house, and in this case they became instruments of revenge. One day while her husband was away, Bergthora sent a servant to cut wood in one of Iceland's few remaining forests, owned jointly by Njal and Gunnar and long shared by them amicably. When Hallgerd heard of it, she concluded that Bergthora was trying to rob her and ordered her overseer to kill the slave. Hallgerd made no attempt to hide the deed—to take a life without admitting it was the gravest and most contemptible offense any Icelander could commit. Instead, she sent word of the killing to Gunnar at the Althing, and he laid the matter before Njal and offered to pay his friend any compensation he demanded.

"You will find it hard to compensate for all the damage Hallgerd will cause," Njal foretold. But he was not about to let the incident spoil their friendship and exacted the minimum fine for a slave's death, 12 ounces of silver. His wife deemed that grossly insufficient and imposed her own stiff penalty, sending a servant to murder the overseer—an act Njal atoned for by returning to Gunnar the 12 ounces of silver. Predictably, Hallgerd was unappeased and kept the feud going. One killing followed another, claiming the lives of men of higher status connected to the two households and forcing Gunnar and Njal to pay much steeper fines, even as they reiterated their vows of friendship. More than once, Gunnar's wife tried to goad him into joining in the feud, but he kept faith with Njal.

Gunnar was not entirely immune to his wife's criticism. Her passion for vengeance was shared by more than a few of her fellow Icelanders, who measured a man's courage by his readiness to repay in-

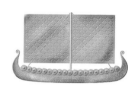

drawn into a feud with Oktel, who refused to accept the compensation Gunnar offered and instead summoned him to court on charges of theft—a disgraceful crime in Iceland, where goods were scarce, and one that brought more shame on the accused than a confessed killing. Njal intervened on Gunnar's behalf and managed to resolve the matter without a trial. But Gunnar deeply resented being called a thief, and when Oktel later challenged him to combat, Gunnar raised his halberd and cut the man down. Far from exulting, he wondered aloud to a companion why the bloody deeds that others reveled in offered him so little satisfaction. Was he "any the less manly than other men," he wondered, for being more reluctant than they were to kill?

Whether he liked it or not, Gunnar was now

"You are an evil woman, and your shame will long be remembered."

sults and exact blood for blood. By such standards, Gunnar appeared weak. He was willing to accept that as the price of preserving a treasured friendship, but he would not be so patient when others challenged him, even if his wife provoked them to it. On one fateful occasion, Hallgerd sent a slave to steal food from a well-stocked neighbor named Oktel, who had refused to share provisions with them during a famine. When Gunnar questioned her about the incident, she lashed out at her prying husband. "It's not a man's business to bother about kitchen matters," she snapped. Gunnar replied that he had no intention of becoming a "thief's accomplice" and slapped her in the face—an act that had doomed two men before him and that Hallgerd promised to remember and repay.

Although Gunnar knew his wife was at fault, he was soon

caught up in a relentless cycle of violence. "This will be the start of your career of killing," Njal warned, knowing well that the victim's powerful kin would seek vengeance. There was danger on the horizon for Njal as well. Having survived strife between their households and strengthened their bonds, the two men were now so closely linked that Gunnar's enemies would inevitably become Njal's as well.

As Njal predicted, Gunnar faced repeated challenges in the months and years ahead. He always prevailed in combat, but every victory widened his circle of foes. Njal did his best to appease the bereaved kin by arranging for the appropriate compensation, but more and more men of influence were turning against Gunnar. Finally, a powerful chieftain who had lost more than one relative to Gunnar brought charges against him at the Althing that stuck.

Here at Iceland's majestic Godafoss (Waterfall of the Gods), the law-speaker Thorgeir reportedly tossed idols of the Norse gods into the water around the year 1000 in order to confirm his decree at the Althing endorsing Christianity as the official religion.

Gunnar was outlawed for three years, meaning that he would have to leave the country for that period or risk execution at the hands of his enemies, who could strike at him with impunity.

Reluctantly, Gunnar readied himself for exile. As he was riding down to the harbor to embark, however, his horse stumbled, forcing him to the ground, and he took the opportunity to look back at all he was leaving behind. "How lovely the slopes are," he remarked, "more lovely than they have ever seemed to me before, golden corn-fields and new-mown hay." He turned his horse about and returned to a place he cherished more than his life.

Unlike some outlaws who chose to remain in their home-land, Gunnar did not go into hiding. After all, he had been sore-ly provoked by his enemies and saw no reason to skulk about like a criminal. But his open defiance of the Althing's sentence made him easy prey. In the end, his enemies surrounded him at home in the night. He held them at bay with his bow until his string broke, then turned to his wife in desperation and asked for a few locks of her long hair to twine together as a makeshift bowstring. "My life depends on it," he told her, but the unforgiving Hall-gerd reminded him of the slap on the face he had given her years before and abandoned him to his fate. Gunnar's sorrowful moth-er pronounced the ultimate judgment on her conduct: "You are an evil woman, and your shame will long be remembered."

Njal grieved the loss deeply, and his eldest son was quick to avenge Gunnar's death. Ultimately, attackers descended on Njal's house in the night much as they had on Gunnar's and burned the building down with the occupants trapped inside—an old but nonetheless disreputable custom among feuding Vikings. Unlike Hallgerd, Njal's wife stood by her husband. Offered a chance to leave the flaming building with the other women and children, Bergthora stoutly declined. "I have promised we would share the same fate," she reminded Njal as she lay down beside him. When they died in the flames with their sons, the hopes Njal had long harbored for peace and order in his homeland seemed to perish as well. As he himself had prophesied bleakly in recent days, "Our land will be formed with laws but smashed through lawlessness."

The tumultuous events related in *Njal's Saga* spanned the period when Christianity was introduced to Iceland and became the official religion there, much to the dismay of pagans, as Christians labeled those attached to the old beliefs. Njal himself, born a pagan, readily

RECKONING WITH CHRISTIANITY

The Vikings were reluctant to abandon their traditional beliefs in favor of Christianity. Even when they officially accepted the new faith, as Icelanders did at the Althing, they retained certain elements of the old Norse religion and incorporated its themes into their sacred images and lore.

The conflict between Christianity and the ancestral beliefs began at the dawn of the Viking age. Despite their mercenary attacks on monasteries, some Norsemen were curious about Christianity and receptive to it, but few were inclined to worship Christ exclusively, at the expense of Odin, Thor, or other Norse gods. When the monk

Ansgar set up a mission in Birka, Sweden, in 829, he made a number of converts, profiting by the protection of the Swedish king, who hoped to promote trade and make foreigners feel at home. One Christian relic harbored in Sweden was the silver cross above, discovered in a grave at Birka. Most Vikings of the day saw such crosses as treasures or curiosities, however, and put more faith in Thor's hammer and other pagan symbols.

Not until Norse kings pledged themselves exclusively to Christianity and pressed their followers to do the same did the religion come to predominate among the Vikings. According to legend, King Harald Bluetooth of Denmark renounced paganism and embraced Christianity around 960, after a visiting Ger-

Proof that the Vikings could accommodate more than one faith, this mold was used by an artisan to turn out both Christian crosses and Thor's hammers (left, center).

A 12th-century Swedish tapestry portrays men in the tower of a Christian church ringing bells to ward off monsters of the sort feared by the Vikings during pagan times.

Constructed of wooden staves in the 12th century, this handsome Christian church in Borgund, Norway, is adorned both with crosses and with animal-headed finials inspired by Norse mythology.

"King Harald had this monument made in memory of his father Gorm and his mother Thyri. Harald who won all Denmark and Norway and made the Danes Christians."

King Harald Bluetooth proclaims his faith on this gilded relief from a Christian church in Denmark.

man bishop named Poppo proved the power of his faith by donning red-hot iron gloves and emerging unscathed. King Harald may also have been motivated to convert by more practical concerns, including his desire to improve relations with the German emperor, Otto. In any case, he declared Christianity the one true faith in Denmark and put up the stone at left, portraying Christ on the cross, to show his belief.

The conversion of Norway owed much to Olaf Haraldsson. Though not the first Norwegian monarch to profess Christianity, he promoted the religion with unprecedented zeal, offering those who had not already converted the choice of baptism, exile, or death. Olaf himself perished in 1030 in a battle to retain power, after urging his men on with the exhortation, "Forward, Christ's men, Cross men, King's men!" Not long after his death, the king was canonized as Saint Olaf, the patron saint of Norway—a devout Christian and a dedicated Viking who raised the cross like Thor's hammer and struck down enemies of the faith.

Norway's King Olaf Haraldsson *(lower right)* dies in battle in this illumination from a 14th-century Icelandic manuscript extolling the monarch who became Saint Olaf.

converted to Christianity along with his wife. Before they died, the saga related, they crossed themselves and commended their souls to God. Not all who professed Christianity in Iceland were peace-loving men like Njal, however. Among the pioneering Christian missionaries there was a fiery German priest named Thangbrand, who was hardly one to forgive trespasses or turn the other cheek. Dispatched to Iceland in the late 10th century by King Olaf Tryggvason, Norway's first Christian monarch, Thangbrand made several prominent converts but acquired even more enemies through his relentless attacks on paganism. After a year or two, according to one Icelandic chronicle, the hot-blooded priest went back to Norway in a huff, having by "that time slain here two or three men who had libelled him."

Thangbrand reported to Olaf that most Icelanders were hopelessly opposed to Christianity, and the king retaliated by seizing Icelanders who were visiting Norway and threatening to execute them. Upon learning of their plight, two Icelandic chieftains who had been converted by Thangbrand traveled to Olaf's court and won a reprieve for their countrymen by pledging to return to Iceland with a second priest and to press for the acceptance of Christianity. Once back home, they rallied their fellow converts and brought their case before the Althing. Icelanders devoted to the Norse gods took up arms, and the council grounds nearly became a battle site. After facing each other down, however, the two sides agreed to bring the issue to trial. Convening at the Law Rock, the Christians and the pagans each brought forth witnesses who swore that theirs was the true faith and refused to be bound by the laws of their opponents.

The task of choosing between them fell to Thorgeir, the lawspeaker, a pagan who was nonetheless respected by Christians for his fairness and sagacity. After listening to both sides, the chronicle related, Thorgeir "lay down and spread his cloak over himself, and rested all that day and the next night, nor did he speak a word." As he lay there, he may well have pondered the uncertain future of his people if they continued to defy the ruler of Norway, which was their motherland and mainstay. Of one thing Thorgeir was sure. Iceland could not live by two laws. "If we sunder the laws," he proclaimed before announcing his verdict, "we will also sunder the peace." Thorgeir had both sides swear to abide by his decision. Then he ruled that Iceland would henceforth be a Christian country and that all of its people would have to submit to baptism.

As a concession to the pagans, he specified that "people might sacrifice to the heathen gods secretly, if they wished," and that they would be subject to punishment only if others witnessed their rites and testified against them. Such tolerance did not last long. Within a few years, all heathen observances, whether public or private, were outlawed in Iceland, although secret rites were not easily abolished among a people who cherished their independence and resisted intrusions.

The coming of Christianity certainly did not prevent Icelanders from preserving their old lore or celebrating the virtues of their pagan ancestors. After all, early settlers like Ingolf, who founded Reykjavik, had been as devout in their fashion as any of their Christian descendants. One Icelandic saga composed in Christian times offered an admiring portrait of a pagan chieftain and priest called Thorolf Mostur-Beard, whose first name signaled his devotion to the god Thor. Thorolf had immigrated to Iceland not long after Ingolf and chosen his homestead in a similar manner—by tossing into the sea the pillars from a high seat, carved with an image of Thor. He found the pillars along the shore of a headland known subsequently as Thor's Ness and built

Vikings in Iceland as well as Greenland hunted the hulking walrus *(left)* for its prized tusks and exported much of the ivory to workshops in Europe, where it was carved into precious objects, including crucifixes, miniature altars, and other sacred artifacts. The walrus-ivory crosier at right was found in a bishop's grave in Greenland and may have been crafted there or imported.

a house there for his family and a temple dedicated to Thor.

Inside the temple with its gabled roof stood a raised platform that served as an altar, surrounded by statues of the gods. When presiding there as priest, Thorolf stood at the altar holding a bowl containing the blood of sacrificed animals and used a twig to sprinkle the sacred blood on the altar, the walls, and the worshipers. Through such rites the early settlers experienced the invigorating power and majesty of their gods, much as Christian converts later communed with their Lord by drinking the symbolic blood of the holy wine at Mass.

Thorolf collected taxes from each farmer in his district to support the temple. Among the precious objects he kept in the sanctuary was a ring weighing more than a pound. Thorolf carried this ring to the local assembly he presided over, and all those who testified there had to swear an oath on it. To Thorolf, the council grounds were as sacred as the temple. Such was his reverence for the meeting place, the saga related, that he would not allow anybody to desecrate it "either with bloodshed or with excrement." Those who needed to "ease themselves" had to repair to a rocky isle along the coast called Dirt Skerry. The arrangement was far from convenient for those who flocked to the assembly, but such was Thorolf's prestige that for as long as he lived, no one dared to defy his prohibition.

After his death, however, members of a rival family let it be known that they did not intend "to waste any more shoe-leather on trips to an off-shore skerry whenever they felt the demands of nature." Thorolf's son prevented them from carrying out that crude threat by force of arms, but in blocking one form of desecration he caused another, for blood was spilled and defiled the council grounds. The incident did not bode well for Thorolf's descendants. They would face fierce opposition in the years ahead and would have to fight and scrape to maintain their authority. Thorolf's great-grandson, Snorri the Priest, accepted Christianity and helped promote the new faith, but his conversion did little to alter his combative nature—the name Snorri meant "trouble." While serving as a Christian priest, he continued to engage in feuds and to plot against his enemies. Outwardly, Icelanders like Snorri accepted the Christian gospel as law and paid lip service to its lessons of forbearance and humility, but inwardly they remained proud, imperious, and prone to lawlessness.

In Iceland, as elsewhere in the Viking world, people had strong precedent for adhering to their truculent ways and defying authorities. After all, some of the great figures in Viking history had been lawbreakers who were ousted from their homelands and found fresh opportunities abroad for themselves and for thousands of others who followed in their wake. Without such ambitious troublemakers, the Vikings would never have achieved as much as they did. And that restless urge to skirt the law and seek freedom and fortune elsewhere lived on. By the time Christianity came to Iceland, a small band of pioneers had already sailed west to a new country, led by an outlaw who harnessed his hostile energies and broke fresh ground in one of the harshest settings Vikings ever encountered.

His name was Erik the Red, and he lived up to his title in every respect, boasting a ruddy complexion, fiery hair, and a bloody temper. Born in Norway around 950, he came of violent stock. Both he and his father were forced to leave their homeland "because of some killings," one saga related matter-of-factly, as if the circumstances were too commonplace to bear repeating. He continued his murderous ways in Iceland, where he

assembled a formidable fighting band to prosecute a feud with a neighbor. In 982 Erik and his henchmen were outlawed for three years. Despite his recklessness, or perhaps because of it, Erik had powerful admirers, several of whom sheltered him from his enemies and helped equip the outlaws for a lengthy journey abroad.

Having exhausted his welcome in both Norway and Iceland,

Emigrants from Iceland set up camp after reaching Greenland in this portrayal of the tasks awaiting the newcomers—including raising tents, preparing meals from grain they brought with them and from fish caught there *(upper left)*, tending their hungry livestock, and repairing their ships.

RICHARD SCHLECHT

Erik longed for a world of his own, and he thought he knew where to find one. Earlier in the century, an Icelandic mariner sailing home from Norway had been caught in a gale that blew his vessel several hundred miles past Iceland to the west, where he briefly sighted a mysterious landmass in the distance. Erik and his crew set out to find and reconnoiter that unknown country. After several days at sea they came upon a forbidding coastline, sheathed in ice, and sailed south in search of more promising terrain. They spent their first harrowing winter near the southern tip of what proved to be an immense island. The following summer they explored an inviting fjord along the southwest coast, graced with tranquil harbors and grassy verges, and built a house there that sheltered them for the remainder of their exile. Winters were harsher here than in Iceland. Chill winds ushered in one snowstorm after another. Gray skies hid the sun during the few precious hours of daylight. This was no paradise, but it was Erik's land, and he would make the most of it.

Once his banishment had expired, Erik returned to Iceland, but only long enough to retrieve his wife and enlist recruits for a colony on the coast he had scouted. He called the place Greenland, knowing that people "would be much more eager to go there if the land had an attractive name." In truth, the pasturage was sparse compared with the endless expanses of snow and ice. But Erik's knack for promoting the place—combined with the fact that all the good country in Iceland had been claimed—prompted enough enthusiasm to fill 25 ships with immigrants, along with their livestock and household items. Led by Erik, they left Iceland on a pleasant breeze in the summer of 986 but soon encountered storm winds on the open sea. One vessel after another foundered or turned back. In the end, 14 ships reached Greenland, carrying some 400 exhausted colonists.

Further travails awaited the first settlers in their new home. The grassy strips that they chose for their settlements were located well up the fjords, sometimes right against glaciers, which shifted periodically, with devastating effect on the stone houses and huts of the settlers. The summers were too short and bleak to allow for substantial grain harvests. People subsisted mainly on fish and on the flesh and milk of their gaunt cattle and sheep. Like the Icelanders, they depended on visiting merchant ships for such necessities as timber and iron. In return, they offered the merchants wool and more exotic items culled at great effort in far northern Greenland—including walrus tusks and skins and down from the nests of eider ducks. Those were the same prizes as the ones gathered in the Arctic regions of Scandinavia, and the Greenlanders who went after them lived a rugged, roving existence, much like the Lapps whom the Norwegian merchant Ottar had trafficked with during the ninth century.

Christianity came to Greenland not long after it reached Iceland, but the new faith did not immediately sweep away the old beliefs and superstitions. People still saw ghosts at night and looked for charms to counter their evil spells. In seasons of misfortune, Greenlanders consulted prophets or seeresses to learn how much longer their ordeal would last. Early in the 11th century, one saga related, Greenland was racked by famine, and "men who had gone out fishing caught poor catches, and some never came back." People knew that if they consumed all their livestock, they would have nothing to live on in the future. They were desperate to learn when the hard times would end. One prominent farmer sent for a seeress named Thorbjorg, the last survivor of a brood of 10 sisters versed in the occult arts.

"This is the kind of proceeding I feel I cannot assist in, for I am a Christian woman."

Some of the settlers may have been disappointed by the stringent country Erik brought them to, but they did not reject his leadership. In the rigors of this new land, the former outlaw became a pillar of the community. He reportedly enjoyed "high distinction, and all recognized his authority." The settlers needed a strong hand to guide them, and Erik did not offend them by trying to set himself up as a tyrant. Indeed, Greenlanders soon convened a national assembly much like Iceland's Althing and adopted similar laws. Their colony proved stable enough to attract other emigrants from Iceland. By the end of the 11th century, some 3,000 people were living on 100 or so farms along the fjords of Greenland's southwest coast.

She arrived in a costume that signaled to all on hand that this was a woman of remarkable properties. She wore "a blue cloak with straps, which was set with stones right down to the hem." She had glass beads around her neck—precious imports that reached Greenland from as far away as Venice—and carried a wooden staff ornamented with brass and gems. No less impressive were the pelts and furs she wore, as if invoking the powers of the animal kingdom. Her shoes were made of hairy calfskin, her hood of black lambskin lined with white catskin, and her gloves of the same catskin with the fur inside, warming her fingers. She carried the tools of her trade, her magic charms, in a large hide pouch fastened to her belt. Her host did her the hon-

or of offering her the high seat at the table, making sure to place a cushion stuffed with hen's feathers there. She ate what little her host could offer her with her own utensils—a brass spoon and a knife with an ivory handle made of walrus tusk.

When it came time to tell the future, Thorbjorg sought the help of other experienced women, familiar with the chants that enhanced divination. Unfortunately, no one in attendance claimed such knowledge with the exception of a young maiden named Gudrid. She confessed that she had learned a magical chant from her foster mother back in Iceland, but she was reluctant to participate. "This is the kind of proceeding I feel I cannot assist in," she explained, "for I am a Christian woman."

Thorbjorg pressed her gently, "It might happen that you could prove helpful to folk in this affair, and still be no worse a woman than before." Gudrid did not want to offend the assembled guests or her host, who had arranged the divination, and at length she agreed. Forming a circle with the other women around Thorbjorg, Gudrid chanted in such a beautiful voice that Thorbjorg credited her with luring spirits who had been keeping their distance but now drew close to lend ear to the lovely song. Inspired by their presence, Thorbjorg discerned the future clearly and informed her host that the

AN OUTPOST IN THE NEW WORLD

Around AD 1000 Vikings arrived at L'Anse aux Meadows on the coast of Newfoundland and built turf-covered houses like those reconstructed at the site (above). This outpost dates from the time of Leif Eriksson, who sailed west from Greenland and wintered at a place he named Vinland, or Wineland, for its grapes. Other Greenlanders later settled there briefly, meeting fierce opposition from native people they called Skraelings.

In some respects L'Anse aux Meadows fits the description of Vinland, but the area lacks the grapes found in milder climes to the south. Perhaps Leif was referring to other berries that could be made into wine—or perhaps he was exaggerating the bounty of the place by naming it Vinland, much as his father, Erik the Red, did in the case of Greenland.

"famine will not last longer than this winter, and that the season will mend when spring comes." She foresaw great things for Gudrid, as well, declaring that she would make the most distinguished match in Greenland.

According to the saga, Thorbjorg's prophecies were fulfilled: "Little indeed of what she said failed to come about." Gudrid's father, however, a devout Christian, was so offended by the divination that he refused to remain in a house where such "heathendom" was being practiced. But he was not sorry to see the pagan prophecy borne out in regard to his daughter, for whom he had long harbored high expectations. As promised, Gudrid indeed made a brilliant match by marrying Thorstein Eriksson, the son of Greenland's founder.

Erik had another son, Leif Eriksson, who carried on his father's tradition in the early 11th century by sailing west with a band of explorers. It was the first of several ventures that fostered a short-lived colony at a place Leif named Vinland. Like Erik's pioneering journey to Greenland, Leif's voyage to Vinland was inspired by the report of a sailor who lost his way in a storm. In 986 the Icelander Bjarni Herjolfsson was en route to Greenland when a northeasterly gale carried him far past his destination and brought him within sight of a well-forested land. Bjarni was in no mood to explore and headed back to Greenland by a route that carried him past other bleak shores, none of which tempted him to make landfall. Fifteen years later, however, Leif Eriksson set out to retrace Bjarni's route in search of a promising place to settle. By one account, Erik meant to accompany Leif but fell from his horse on his way to embark and had to remain behind. "I am not meant to discover more countries than this one we are now in," he told his son. "This is as far as we go together."

Leif's journey brought him first to a dismal place of rocks and glaciers he called Helluland (Baffin Island) and thence to a country he dubbed Markland (Labrador), distinguished by dense forests. From there, Leif and his crew sailed south to Vinland, where they spent the winter. Vinland owed its name to the grapes that reportedly grew there in abundance, but that was just one of its attractions. The salmon in the lakes and streams "were bigger than any others the men had ever seen," one saga related, and the winter there was mild and bright compared with Greenland: "On the shortest day of winter the sun remained up between breakfast time and late afternoon." Leif and his crew may well have wintered on the north coast of Newfoundland, where the foundations of a Viking outpost were later uncovered. But if Vinland was indeed a place of grapevines and balmy winters, it may have been located farther to the southwest, perhaps even along the coast of New England.

Even when the climate turned colder after 1200, Greenlanders continued to wear European-style garments like this woolen hood and dress, found buried in a grave in the frozen turf. The Inuit, or Eskimos, fared better in their hides and furs and outlasted the Norse colonists in Greenland.

The next spring Leif and his men returned to Greenland. He had hoped to lead settlers to Vinland himself, but shortly after his return his father died, and he assumed Erik's responsibilities at home. It fell to others to attempt the colonization of Vinland. They might have succeeded had the land been uninhabited. But instead the colonists, whose ranks included a number of women, met with native people they called Skraelings and clashed with them. By 1020 the last of those discouraged pioneers had returned to Greenland.

Vinland marked the farthest known advance in the phenomenal westward surge of the Vikings. Thereafter, their energies would ebb, and the North Atlantic colonies would have a hard time supporting themselves. Ultimately, in the 13th century, amid a worsening climate and mounting strife, the beleaguered settlers in both Greenland and Iceland would surrender their coveted independence and attach themselves to Norway.

The glory of the Vikings was gone but not forgotten. Even as Icelanders prepared to abolish their free state and pledge fealty to the Norwegian king, they were setting down in writing the remarkable sagas that would preserve for posterity the dreams and deeds of their irrepressible Norse ancestors. The most prolific of the saga writers, Snorri Sturluson, was born to one of Iceland's leading families in 1179 and schooled in both the law and the lore of his land. In a hectic career that harked back to the adventures of the Vikings he wrote about, he served twice as Iceland's lawspeaker, feuded with political rivals, traveled to Norway and regaled the king and his court with tales of their royal predecessors, and returned late in his life to Iceland, where a powerful chieftain whom he had earlier antagonized was lying in wait for him. On the night of September 23, 1241, dozens of armed men broke into Snorri's house, chased him from his bed into the cellar, and murdered the man who did more than any other to uphold the Norse legacy. Like others versed in the law, he fell prey to lawlessness, but his sagas lived on, testifying to the powerful creative impulse that flourished in the Viking world amid the forces of destruction.

PRIZED POSSESSIONS

Though seen as barbarians by the Europeans whose treasures they plundered, the Vikings had a finely honed love of beautiful things. Indeed, their desire for the thick brocades, fine silks, and precious metals and gems to be found so many miles from home fueled the Vikings' travels in spite of the attendant hardships of hunger, fighting, and sometimes, death.

When Viking marauders and traders returned home with their booty, Norse craftspeople wasted no time putting their own individual stamp on it. Coins, jewelry, and crucifixes alike were melted down to produce new pieces with a distinctly Viking style. Almost all Viking art was applied art, or the decoration of functional objects, and on some extravagantly embellished pieces, made for the rich or famous, hardly a surface went unadorned. But even average men and women seemed drawn to add some color to their daily lives, using their idle hours to beautify such homely items as fishline winders.

The Vikings themselves apparently thought of their warriors as fearsome figures. An example of fine Viking woodcarving, this rare portrayal of a human face adorned a wagon entombed in the Oseberg ship burial.

A finely worked silver amulet representing Thor's hammer also incorporates the staring eyes and eagle's beak associated with the god.

Intricately carved ribbonlike creatures intertwine on this wooden post, one of five that were discovered in the Oseberg site. The Vikings probably used these animal-head posts, with their staring eyes and fierce demeanors, in religious ceremonies.

A WARRIOR'S FLOURISHES

"He always went around in a scarlet tunic with a grey fur cloak over it, a bearskin cap on his head, and a sword in his hand. . . . He called this sword 'Leg-Biter', and he never let it out of his sight."

An eagle, the Viking bird of battle, adorns a gilt-bronze harness mount.

An ornately decorated harness bow features intricate inlaid spiral designs and animal motifs of gilded copper and silver. The harness bow, a Danish invention, was used to keep a horse's reins from tangling, by passing them through a hole in the bow's center.

Silver inlays and a band of gold cover an iron battle-ax head that was buried with a Danish Viking. Kings and chieftains sometimes gave such elaborately ornamented axes to warriors as rewards for service.

The hilt of this iron double-edged sword found in a Hedeby boat burial is trimmed with gilt bronze and encrusted with silver. The silver is separated into blocks by silver wire and inset with decorative motifs outlined in niello, a black enamel-like substance.

DOMESTIC TREASURES

Beasts with teeth bared enliven a whalebone board used by Norwegian women for smoothing linen or making pleats in garments. More than 40 of these prized boards have been found in the graves of wealthy Viking women.

Even a tool as mundane as a whale-bone fishline winder was beautified by a Viking artisan with incised circular designs and the image of a plump bird.

Crosshatching and inter-laced designs embellish a bone pin used to fasten a dress. The wearer secured the pin to her clothing with a cord or leather thong passed through the perforation.

"A homestead is better,
though it be small
—everyone is a hero at home;
though one owns two goats
and a rope-raftered croft,
that is still better
than begging."

DAZZLING ADORNMENTS

Embossed figures outlined with filigree
and filled in with gold grains cover the
top and sides of this drum-shaped brooch
that would have been worn on the breast
to fasten a woman's outer garment.

*"Gudrun was betrothed to Thorvald. . . .
Thorvald was also to buy precious things
for her, so that no woman of comparable
wealth should own finer jewelry
than Gudrun."*

Cast in a single molded piece, this massive, solid silver armlet would have been beautiful but very heavy to wear. Viking silversmiths often made jewelry from melted-down Arab coins.

A Viking craftsperson fashioned 32 silver and gilt-bronze fish with mouths agape and strung them together to form this unusual necklace. Both men and women loved the ornate jewelry that was made from precious metals brought home from raids or trading expeditions.

A bronze ring-brooch, used to fasten a man's cloak at the shoulder, incorporates three Viking heads into its design.

GLOSSARY

Aesir: a family of gods and goddesses who lived in Asgard, two of the most important being Odin and Thor.

Afi: the name of the male occupant of the farmhouse where Rig stayed when he visited earth. Also called Grandfather.

Ai: the name of the male occupant of the hut where Rig stayed when he visited earth. Also called Great-Grandfather.

All-Father: another name for Odin.

Althing: in Iceland, originally the annual national assembly of the country's landowning chieftains that met for two weeks each summer; first convened in 930 to create and administer a legal code, today it consists of elected members.

Amma: the female occupant of the farmhouse where Rig stayed when he visited earth. Amma, also called Grandmother, bore Rig's son, Karl, or Freeman.

Animal-head posts: elaborately carved wooden posts topped by snarling monster heads with bared teeth or fangs. Only a few have been found; their meaning and use are unknown.

Armlets: bands worn on the arm for ornament or identification; arm rings.

Asgard: the dwelling place and fortress of the Aesir, who lived there in magnificent palaces; located above Midgard and accessible only by the rainbow bridge, Bifrost.

Auger: a tool, similar to a corkscrew, used to bore holes in wood or ice.

A-viking: term used by Norsemen to refer to their raiding voyages and other exploits.

Balder: shining god of light, the beloved son of Odin and Frigg, slain by the treachery of Loki. Balder was one of the few gods who would be resurrected after Ragnarok.

Berserk: a shape changer, also called a bear shirt or a wolf skin; one of a band of premedieval and medieval Norse warriors who wore animal skins and were legendary for their savagery and reckless frenzy in battle.

Blubber: a thick layer of fat between the skin and muscles of whales or other marine mammals, from which oil was derived.

Bondi: in Norway, a landowner, or farmer.

Bride price: money or goods given to the family of the bride by the bridegroom or his family.

Byzantines: those who lived in or near the ancient city of Byzantium, later Constantinople, and today Istanbul, Turkey.

Caftan: in the Middle East, a man's loose, ankle-length garment that opens at the front, with long, wide sleeves, usually worn with a sash.

Chain mail: flexible armor made of metal links or scales. Also called mail.

Chieftain: the leader of a band, tribe, or clan; a jarl.

Clinker built: a method of shipbuilding employed in medieval northern Europe using an overlapping pattern to join the planks in a ship's hull.

Concubine: a secondary wife, often with few legal rights and low social status.

Crosier: a staff with a cross or sphere on the top.

Danegeld: a tax levied in England from the late 10th to the mid-11th century as tribute to the Danish invaders.

Danelaw: the land in the northern, central, and eastern part of England colonized and held by Danes from the ninth through the 11th centuries; the body of customary law, distinctly different from English law, that was in force in the area while it was held by the Danes.

Doom of the Gods: another name for Ragnarok.

Dowry: the property a wife or her family gives to her husband upon marriage.

Dragon ships: name for the largest of the longships, decorated with dragon heads on their prows and used for raiding, warfare, and exploration.

Drekar: another name for dragon ships.

Edda: the name of the female occupant of the hut where Rig stayed when he visited earth, and the mother of his son, Thrall. She was also known as Great-Grandmother.

Ell: a measure of cloth, the length of which varied.

Father: the male occupant of the great hall where Rig stayed when he visited earth.

Fealty: an oath and procedure of recognition of the fidelity and assistance owed by a vassal to his lord and the protection owed by the lord to the vassal, an obligation that passed from one generation to the next.

Fenrir: a demon wolf, symbol of death and destruction. Also known as Fenris, or Fenris-wolf.

Finnas: another name for the native Lapps who inhabit an area of Scandinavia largely within the Arctic Circle.

Fjord: a long, deep, narrow arm of the sea between steep slopes, usually extending far inland.

Fosterage: in Norway, the entrusting by the king or a noble of his children to another, inferior to him in rank, to be raised.

Freeman: a person not in slavery; one who possesses the rights and privileges of a citizen; Rig's son, also called Karl, by the mortal called Grandmother, or Amma.

Frey: god of fertility and peace, sunshine and rain, and prosperity. Brother of Freya.

Freya: goddess of fertility, love, battle, and death, in the last capacity claiming half of all warriors who fell in battle. Sister of Frey.

Frigg: the supreme goddess; goddess of marriage; wife of Odin, mother of Balder.

Frost giants: a class of giants.

Futhark: the Viking runic alphabet, named for the first six characters and consisting of 16 runes, each of which represents a sound in the spoken language and which also has a name and meaning of its own.

Gall-Gaedhil: an Irish faction which, according to legend, renounced Christianity and joined the Norwegians in their pagan rites. Also called Foreign Gaels.

Gangplank: a board or ramp used as a bridge between a ship and a pier.

Giants: also called frost giants. Evil inhabitants of Jotunheim; the personification of destruction and chaos, who possessed superhuman powers. The enemies of humans and gods.

Godafoss: "Waterfall of the Gods." A waterfall in northern Iceland where an early chieftain, converted to Christianity, cast off pagan idols.

Godi: in Iceland, a title meaning priest-chieftain. The godi maintained order and convened local courts to resolve disputes within his jurisdiction.

Halberd: a weapon combining both a spear and a battle-ax on a stout pole.

Heimdall: the watchman of the gods who lived near and guarded the rainbow bridge into Asgard. Also called Rig.

Hel: goddess of death who ruled over Niflheim.

Helluland: "Flat Stone Land." Leif Eriksson's name for Baffin Island.

Helmsman: one who steers a ship.

Housecarl: a member of the personal or household troops of medieval Scandinavian kings and chieftains.

Hrungnir: one of the frost giants.

Inuit: any of the native Eskimo peoples of North America, especially those of arctic Canada and Greenland.

Jarl: a medieval Scandinavian chieftain or nobleman, equivalent to an English earl; Rig's son by the mortal called Mother, and the father of the ruling class of nobles. Through his son Kon, Jarl was also considered to be the father of Norse royalty.

Jester: a comic entertainer whose real or feigned madness or imbecility made him a source of amusement at medieval courts.

Jotunheim: "Home of the Giants." The mountainous, freezing land across the ocean where the frost giants lived.

Juggler: an entertainer who performs feats or tricks of manual dexterity.

Karl: in Scandinavia, a freeman; Rig's son by the

mortal called Grandmother, or Amma. Karl, also known as Freeman, was considered to be the father of the Viking class of freemen.

Keel: in shipbuilding, the main structural member, the backbone of the ship, running lengthwise along the center of the bottom of the hull from stem to stern.

Kenning: in skaldic verse, a figurative, usually compound phrase, replacing a common noun; a metaphor.

Kirtle: a man's snug, knee-length tunic.

Knorr: a Viking merchant ship, shorter, bulkier, and wider than the dragon-headed longships, with a central, open cargo hold used for transporting people and goods.

Kon (Kon ungr): the name of the favorite son of Jarl. Kon was considered to be the progenitor of Norse royalty and nobility, and the name came to mean king.

Law Rock: the prominence at Thingvellir upon which the lawspeaker stood each summer to recite Iceland's judicial code.

Lawspeaker: in medieval Scandinavia, the local official who was learned in the unwritten law and who presided over the *thing;* in Iceland, the chieftain who pronounced the letter of the law in cases of doubt and who recited the law once a year before the Althing.

Liegeman: a feudal vassal or subject; a loyal supporter or follower.

Loki: a giant who lived among the Aesir; the cunning god of mischief, discord, and strife, and the force behind Balder's death. The father of Hel, Fenrir, and the World Serpent.

Longhouse: a communal residence with one to three rooms, 40 to 100 feet long, sometimes with stables, storage sheds, and workshops attached.

Longships: a type of clinker-built ship with a single sail and a continuous row of oars on each side, used by the Vikings for warfare, raiding parties, and explorations.

Markland: "Wood Land"; Leif Eriksson's name for Newfoundland.

Mast: a tall, vertical pole in the center of a ship, from which sails hang.

Mead: an alcoholic beverage made by fermenting honey and water.

Midgard: in the Norse universe, the world of humans, midway between Asgard and Niflheim, connected to Asgard by the rainbow bridge, and surrounded by the ocean where the World Serpent lived.

Mjollnir: Thor's great, magical hammer and a symbol of his power.

Moraine: an accumulation of boulders, stones, sand, or other debris carried and deposited by a glacier.

Mosque: any house or area of prayer in Islam.

Mother: the name of the female occupant of the great hall where Rig stayed when he visited earth. Mother was the mortal who bore Rig's son, Jarl.

Nabidh: an alcoholic brew.

Niello: a black metallic alloy used to fill designs engraved on the surface of an object made of a different metal.

Niflheim: "mist home." In the Norse universe, the home of those who died of old age or disease; the dark, misty region of eternal cold and night, ruled by the goddess Hel.

Normandy: an area in France that derived its name from the Norsemen who settled there in great numbers.

Normans: name given to the Scandinavian people who in the 10th century settled in the area of France that became Normandy.

Norse: of or relating to medieval Scandinavia or its people, languages, culture, and settlements.

Oath helpers: at the thing, individuals who would testify as to the truthfulness of one of the parties in a dispute.

Odin: the chief god of the Aesir; the god of war, poetry, wisdom, and death, in the last capacity claiming half of all warriors who fell in battle. Husband of Frigg, father of Thor and Balder.

Parley: a conference, especially one between enemies over terms of a truce.

Picture stones: stone markers carved with elaborate scenes, designs, or depictions of episodes from mythology. Unlike rune-stones, they did not include inscriptions.

Prow: the front of a ship; on Viking ships, often decorated with snarling animal heads.

Quarter things: in Iceland, the name of the four regional councils that settled disputes that a local godi could not resolve.

Quern: a primitive hand-turned device of stone used to grind grain into flour.

Ragnarok: "Doom of the Gods"; the time when evil would be unleashed upon the world, the frost giants and monsters would attack both humanity and the gods, and there would be a cataclysmic struggle in which most of the gods, giants, and demons would be slain. After this apocalyptic battle, the entire universe (except for the World Tree) would be consumed; the earth would sink into the sea, to rise again, purified, and selected gods and worthy humans would be resurrected to live forever.

Regent: one who rules during the minority, absence, or incapacitation of a monarch.

Relics: objects of religious veneration, said to have magical or mystical powers.

Rig: the name Heimdall used when visiting earth. Rig's offspring by mortals became the basis for the three classes of Norse society: slaves, freemen, and nobles.

Rigsthula: an ancient Icelandic poem found in the *Poetic Edda,* which relates the myth of the creation of the three classes of Viking society.

Runes: angular alphabetical characters or symbols, sometimes believed to have magical powers, used by Scandinavians from the third to the 12th centuries.

Rune-stones: stones bearing carved runic inscriptions, erected to commemorate an event or memorialize an individual.

Runic inscriptions: inscriptions, dedicatory or commemorative of some event or person, carved on stone or other durable surfaces.

Rus: ancient people who gave their name to Russia, believed by many scholars to have been the Swedes who traded with the Slavs and settled among them.

Scribe: one who copied down the words of others; a clerk or secretary.

Shape changer: name given to someone with a volatile nature who became easily frenzied, especially in times of danger. A berserk.

Shield wall: a formation in which soldiers stand so close together that even some of those who have been slain remain upright.

Ship burials: the practice in medieval Scandinavia of burying the dead in ships covered by burial mounds or in a grave surrounded by raised stones laid in the shape of a ship.

Shires: in Anglo-Saxon southern England, an administrative division, equivalent to and superseded by the county system after the Norman Conquest.

Sif: Thor's wife.

Skald: a medieval Scandinavian poet, attached to a court or noble household, especially one writing in the Viking age.

Skaldic verse: court poetry originating in Norway but developed chiefly by Icelandic skalds from the ninth to the 13th centuries.

Skerry: a small, low, rocky reef or island.

Skraelings: Leif Eriksson's name for the natives of Greenland and Vinland.

Skyr: fermented milk.

Slaves: thralls; workers of the lowest possible status, with no legal rights and protections.

Slavs: a people native to eastern Europe, enslaved in large numbers by the Vikings.

Sleipnir: Odin's gray, eight-legged horse, who could carry his master over the sea, through the air, and between the realms of the living and the dead.

Snood: a head covering, ribbon, or net worn over

or around the hair of women in many cultures during medieval times.

Soapstone: a soft, easily carved stone used for dishes of various types.

Stem: the curved, main upright beam at the front of a boat.

Stern: the rear part of a ship.

Strandhögg: a coastal raid on farms, settlements, or monasteries for cattle and other property.

Sword: a weapon with a long straight or slightly curved, single- or double-sided blade, set into a hilt.

Thing: in medieval Scandinavia, a local or provincial communal council, the basic unit of government and law; in Iceland, a local public assembly of freemen convened periodically to act as a court in resolving disputes or punishing criminal behavior within a district.

Thingvellir: the meeting place where the Icelandic Althing was held from 930 to 1798, located east of Reykjavik.

Thor: god of thunder; the most widely worshiped of the gods. Thor represented order, law, and stability.

Thrall: in Scandinavia, a slave; Rig's son by the mortal called Edda; the father of the Viking slave class.

Trefoil brooch: in Scandinavia, a three-lobed brooch used to fasten a woman's shawl.

Trolls: misshapen giants who lived in caves or beneath hills, inclined to thievery and kidnapping of children.

Vadmál: a rough, woolen homespun fabric, a Scandinavian medium of exchange.

Valhalla: in Asgard, Odin's hall of slain warriors, where those killed in battle would spend the afterlife drinking, dining, wenching, and fighting until the coming of Ragnarok.

Valkyrie: any of Odin's handmaidens who selected which warriors would die in battle, conducted their souls to Valhalla, and waited upon them there.

Vanir: a family of gods and goddesses, residents of Vanaheim. The Vanir were associated with fertility, peace, and plenty as well as with magic. Members of the Vanir included Frey and Freya.

Varangian guard: a group of soldiers, including many Viking mercenaries, who served the rulers of Byzantium.

Vellum: a thin, supple writing material made of calfskin, lambskin, or kidskin.

Viking age: the period from about 800 to 1100 when Scandinavians engaged in numerous plundering expeditions abroad.

Viking: any of the seafaring Scandinavian people from Denmark, Sweden, and Norway, who plundered the coasts of northern and western Europe from the ninth through the 11th centuries, as well as those who colonized these and other areas. Also called Norsemen.

Vinland: a Viking outpost, also called Wineland. The unidentified coastal area of North America that Leif Eriksson visited about the year 1000, believed to be somewhere between southern Labrador and New Jersey.

Wattle and daub: a method of housing construction in which vertical wooden stakes were interwoven horizontally with twigs, then covered with a mixture of clay or mud.

Wergild: compensation paid by the person committing a crime or offense to the injured party or his survivors; blood money.

Whetstone: a hard stone used to sharpen knives and tools.

World Serpent: the giant serpent who lived in the oceans surrounding Midgard; an enemy of world order. Son of Loki, brother of Fenrir and Hel.

World Tree: another name for Yggdrasil.

Yard: a long crossbar hung from a mast, used to support and spread the top of a square sail.

Yggdrasil: the World Tree, a giant ash that supported and held the universe together. Its roots extended into Asgard, Midgard, and Niflheim, and it bound together heaven, earth, and hell. Although badly shaken, it would survive Ragnarok.

PRONUNCIATION GUIDE

Aesir (AY-seer)
Ai (EYE)
Althing (AHL-thing)
Aud (OHD)
Balder (BAHLD-ur)
Bergthora (BEHRG-thohr-uh)
Bjarni Herjolfsson (BYAHRN-ee HAYR-yawlf-son)
Bjorn (BYERN)
Canute (kuh-NOOT)
Egill Skallagrimsson (AY-gil SKAL-uh-GRIM-son)
Eystein (AY-stayn)
Floki (FLOH-kee)
Freya (FRAY-yuh)
Fyrkat (FEER-kuht)
Gardar (GAHR-dahr)
Godafoss (GAWD-uh-fos)
Gokstad (GAWK-stad)
Guthorm (GOOTH-ohrm)
Gyda (GID-uh)
Haakon Grjotgardson (HAW-kun GROHT-gahrd-son)

Halvdan (HAHLV-dun)
Hallgerd (HAHL-guhrd)
Heimskringla (HAYMS-kring-luh)
Hjorleif (YOHR-layf)
Hrungnir (RUNG-neer)
Hrut (ROOT)
Ingolf Arnarson (ING-golf AHR-nahr-son)
Jarlabanki (YAHRL-la-BAHNK-ee)
Jarl (YAHRL)
Jorvik (YOHR-vik)
Jotunheim (YOHT-uhn-haym)
Kveldulf (KVEL-duhlf)
Leif Eriksson (LAYF EH-rik-son)
Leif Hrodmarsson (LAYF ROHD-mar-son)
Mikligardr (MIK-lih-gahrd-ur)
Mjollnir (MYOHL-neer)
Niflheim (NIV-uhl-haym)
Njal (NYAHL)
Odin (OH-din)
Olaf Tryggvason (OH-luhf TRIG-vuh-son)
Oseberg (OH-suh-burg)

Oslo Fjord (OS-loh fyord)
Ragnarok (RAHG-nuh-rok)
Ragnhild (RAHG-nild)
Reykjavik (RAYK-yuh-vik)
Rigsthula (RIGS-too-luh)
Rognvald (ROG-nah-vahld)
Rolf Ganger (RAWLF GAYNG-ger)
Sleipnir (SLAYP-neer)
Snorri Sturluson (SNOHR-ree STUHR-luh-son)
Svein Ulfsson (SVAYN UHLV-son)
Thangbrand (THAYNG-brand)
Thingvellir (THEENG-vet-leer)
Thor (THOHR)
Thorbjorg (THOHR-byerg)
Thorgeir (THOHR-gayr)
Thorolf (THOHR-rawlf)
Vadmál (VAHD-mahl)
Valkyrie (VAL-keer-ee)
Vestfold (VEST-fohld)
Vifil (VEE-fil)
Yggdrasil (IG-druh-sil)

ACKNOWLEDGMENTS/PICTURE CREDITS

The editors wish to thank the following individuals and institutions for their valuable assistance in the preparation of this volume. The sources for the illustrations that appear in this volume are also listed below. Credits from left to right are separated by semicolons; from top to bottom they are separated by dashes.

ACKNOWLEDGMENTS
Ute Drews, Haithabu Viking Museum/Archäologisches Landesmuseum, Schleswig, Germany; Heidrun Klein, Bildarchiv Preussischer Kulturbesitz, Berlin; Marie Montembault, Département des Antiquités Grecques et Romaines, Musée du Louvre, Paris.

BIBLIOGRAPHY

BOOKS

Adamus Bremensis. *History of the Archbishops of Hamburg-Bremen.* Trans. and ed. by Francis J. Tschan. New York: Columbia University Press, 1959.

Almgren, Bertil, et al. *The Viking.* Gothenburg, Sweden: AB Nordbok, 1975.

Batey, Colleen, et al. *Cultural Atlas of the Viking World.* Ed. by James Graham-Campbell. New York: Facts On File, 1994.

Bessinger, Jess B., and Robert P. Creed, eds. *Franciplegius: Medieval and Linguistic Studies in Honor of Francis Peabody Magoun.* New York: New York University Press, 1965.

Blindheim, Charlotte. *The Viking Age.* Oslo: Universitets Oldsaksamling, 1974.

Byock, Jesse L. *Medieval Iceland: Society, Sagas, and Power.* Berkeley: University of California Press, 1988.

Christensen, Arne Emil. *Guide to the Viking Ship Museum.* Oslo: Universitets Oldsaksamling, 1987.

Civardi, Anne, and James Graham-Campbell. *The Time Traveller Book of Viking Raiders.* London: Usborne Publishing, 1977.

Cohat, Yves. *The Vikings: Lords of the Seas.* London: Thames and Hudson, 1992.

Crossley-Holland, Kevin. *The Norse Myths.* New York: Pantheon Books, 1980.

Crumlin-Pedersen, Ole, Mogens Schou Jorgensen, and Torsten Edgren. "Ships and Travel." In *From Viking to Crusader: The Scandinavians and Europe, 800-1200,* ed. by Else Roesdahl and David M. Wilson. New York: Rizzoli, 1992.

Dasent, George Webbe, trans. *The Story of Burnt Njal.* London: J. M. Dent & Sons, 1960.

Davidson, H. R. Ellis:
Gods and Myths of Northern Europe. Harmondsworth, Middlesex, England: Penguin Books, 1964.
The Road to Hel. Cambridge: Cambridge University Press, 1943.
Scandinavian Mythology. London: Hamlyn, 1983.

Donovan, Frank R. *The Vikings.* New York: American Heritage, 1964.

Edda Sæmundar. *Poems of the Elder Edda.* Trans. by Patricia Terry. Philadelphia: University of Pennsylvania Press, 1990.

Eyrbyggja Saga. Trans. by Paul Schach. Lincoln: University of Nebraska Press, 1959.

Fell, Christine E. "Gods and Heroes of the Northern World." In *The Northern World: The History and Heritage of Northern Europe, AD 400-1100,* ed. by David M. Wilson. New York: Harry N. Abrams, 1980.

Foote, Peter, and David M. Wilson. *The Viking Achievement: The Society and Culture of Early Medieval Scandinavia.* London: Sidgwick & Jackson, 1970.

From Viking to Crusader: The Scandinavians and Europe, 800-1200. Ed. by Else Roesdahl and David M. Wilson. New York: Rizzoli, 1992.

Fury of the Northmen: TimeFrame AD 800-1000 (TimeFrame series). Alexandria, Va.: Time-Life Books, 1988.

Graham-Campbell, James. *The Viking World.* London: Frances Lincoln Publishers, 1980.

Graham-Campbell, James, and Dafydd Kidd. *The Vikings.* London: British Museum Publications, 1980.

Hallberg, Peter. *The Icelandic Saga.* Trans. by Paul Schach. Lincoln: University of Nebraska Press, 1962.

Haywood, John. *The Penguin Historical Atlas of the Vikings.* New York: Penguin Books, 1995.

Hermannsson, Halldór. *Icelandic Manuscripts.* Ithaca, N.Y.: Cornell University Library, 1929.

Hollander, Lee M. *The Skalds: A Selection of Their Poems, with Introductions and Notes.* Princeton, N.J.: Princeton University Press, 1945.

Jansson, Sven B. F. *The Runes of Sweden.* New York: Bedminster Press, 1962.

Jesch, Judith. *Women in the Viking Age.* Woodbridge, Suffolk, England: Boydell Press, 1991.

Jochens, Jenny. *Women in Old Norse Society.* Ithaca, N.Y.: Cornell University Press, 1995.

Jones, Gwyn:
A History of the Vikings. Oxford: Oxford University Press, 1984.
The Norse Atlantic Saga: Being the Norse Voyages of Discovery and Settlement to Iceland, Greenland, America. London: Oxford University Press, 1964.

Jones, Gwyn, ed. and trans. *Eirik the Red and Other Icelandic Sagas.* Oxford: Oxford University Press, 1961.

Klindt-Jensen, Ole. *The World of the Vikings.* Washington, D.C.: Robert B. Luce, 1970.

Kristjánsson, Jónas. *Eddas and Sagas: Iceland's Medieval Literature.* Trans. by Peter Foote. Reykjavik: Hið íslenska bókmenntafélag, 1988.

Laxdæla Saga. Trans. by Magnus Magnusson and Hermann Pálsson. London: Penguin Books, 1969.

Logan, F. Donald. *The Vikings in History.* Totowa, N.J.: Barnes & Noble, 1983.

Magnusson, Magnus:
Viking Expansion Westwards. New York: Henry Z. Walck, 1973.

Hammer of the North. London: Orbis, 1976.

Margeson, Susan M. *Viking.* New York: Alfred A. Knopf, 1994.

Marsden, John. *The Fury of the Northmen: Saints, Shrines and Sea-Raiders in the Viking Age, AD 793-878.* New York: St. Martin's Press, 1993.

Martell, Hazel Mary. *The Vikings.* New York: New Discovery Books, 1991.

Medieval Scandinavia: An Encyclopedia. Ed. by Phillip Pulsiano. New York: Garland, 1993.

Njal's Saga. Trans. by Magnus Magnusson, and Hermann Pálsson. New York: Penguin Books, 1960.

Nørlund, Poul. *Viking Settlers in Greenland: And Their Descendants during Five Hundred Years.* Trans. by W. E. Calvert. New York: Kraus Reprint, 1971.

The Northern World: The History and Heritage of Northern Europe, AD 400-1100. Ed. by David M. Wilson. New York: Harry N. Abrams, 1980.

Nylén, Erik. *Stones, Ships and Symbols.* Stockholm: Gidlunds Bokförlag, 1988.

Page, R. I. *Chronicles of the Vikings: Records, Memorials and Myths.* New York: Barnes & Noble, 1995.

Pálsson, Hermann, and Paul Edwards, trans.:
Egil's Saga. New York: Penguin Books, 1976.
Eyrbyggja Saga. Toronto: University of Toronto Press, 1973.
Seven Viking Romances. London: Penguin Books, 1985.

Pencak, William. *The Conflict of Law and Justice in the Icelandic Sagas.* Amsterdam: Editions Rodopi B.V., 1995.

Phillips-Birt, Douglas. *The Building of Boats.* New York: W. W. Norton & Co., 1979.

Portner, Rudolf. *The Vikings: Rise and Fall of the Norse Sea Kings.* Trans. by Sophie Wilkins. London: St. James Press, 1975.

Randsborg, Klavs. *The Viking Age in Denmark: The Formation of a State.* London: Duckworth, 1980.

Richards, Julian D. *Book of Viking Age England.* London: B. T. Batsford, 1991.

Roesdahl, Else. *The Vikings.* Trans. by Susan M. Margeson and Kirsten Williams. London: Penguin Books, 1987.

Roesdahl, Else, et al. *The Vikings in England.* London: The Anglo-Danish Viking Project, 1981.

Rohan, Michael Scott, and Allan J. Scott. *The Hammer and the Cross.* Oxford: Alder, 1980.

Sagas of the Icelanders: A Book of Essays. Ed. by John Tucker. New York: Garland Publishing, 1989.

Sailing into the Past. Proceedings of the International Seminar on Replicas of Ancient and Medieval Vessels, Roskilde, 1984. Ed. by Ole Crumlin-Pedersen and Max Vinner. Roskilde, Denmark: Viking Ship Museum, 1986.

Sawyer, P. H.:

The Age of the Vikings. New York: St. Martin's Press, 1971.

Kings and Vikings: Scandinavia and Europe, AD 700-1100. New York: Barnes & Noble, 1994.

Schach, Paul. *Icelandic Sagas.* Boston: Twayne Publishers, 1984.

Seven Viking Romances. Trans. by Hermann Pálsson and Paul Edwards. New York: Penguin, 1985.

Simpson, Jacqueline:

Everyday Life in the Viking Age. New York: Dorset Press, 1967.

The Viking World. New York: St. Martin's Press, 1980.

Stenton, Frank, ed. *The Bayeux Tapestry.* London: Phaidon Press, 1965.

Sturluson, Snorri:

Egil's Saga. Trans. and ed. by Gwyn Jones. New York: Twayne, 1960.

From the Sagas of the Norse Kings. Oslo: Dreyers Forlag, 1984.

Heimskringla: The Norse King Sagas. Trans. by Erling Monsen and A. H. Smith. New York: E. P. Dutton & Co., 1979.

King Harald's Saga. Trans. by Magnus Magnusson and Hermann Pálsson. Harmondsworth, Middlesex, England: Penguin Books, 1966.

Sveinsson, Einar Olafur. *Njals Saga: A Literary Masterpiece.* Ed. and trans. by Paul Schach. Lincoln: University of Nebraska Press, 1971.

Thorgilsson, Ari. *The Book of the Icelanders (Íslendingabók),* Vol. 20. Ed. and trans. by Halldór Hermannsson. Ithaca, N.Y.: Cornell University Library, 1930.

Thorvildsen, Knud. *The Viking Ship of Ladby.* Copenhagen: National Museum, 1985.

Turville-Petre, E. O. G.:

Myth and Religion of the North: The Religion of Ancient Scandinavia. London: Weidenfeld and Nicolson, 1964.

Nine Norse Studies. London: Viking Society for Northern Research, 1972.

Scaldic Poetry. Oxford: Clarendon Press, 1976.

Two Voyagers at the Court of King Alfred: The Ventures of Ohthere and Wulfstan. Trans. by Christine E. Fell, ed. by Niels Lund. York, England: William Sessions, 1984.

The Viking. Gothenburg, Sweden: Nordbok, 1975.

Vikings: Raiders from the North (Lost Civilizations series). Alexandria, Va.: Time-Life Books, 1993.

The Vikings in England and in Their Danish Homeland. London: Anglo-Danish Viking Project, 1981.

Viking Ways: On the Viking Age in Sweden. Stockholm: Swedish Institute, 1980.

Wernick, Robert, and the editors of Time-Life Books. *The Vikings* (The Seafarers series). Alexandria, Va.: Time-Life Books, 1979.

Whitelock, Dorothy, ed. *The Anglo-Saxon Chronicle.* London: Eyre and Spottiswoode, 1961.

Wilson, David M. *The Vikings and Their Origins.* London: Thames and Hudson, 1980.

Wise, Terence. *Saxon, Viking and Norman* (Men-at-Arms series). London: Osprey, 1979.

PERIODICALS

LaFay, Howard. "The Vikings." *National Geographic,* April 1970.

Setton, Kenneth M. "900 Years Ago: The Norman Conquest." *National Geographic,* August 1966.

OTHER SOURCES

Tweddle, Dominic, Richard Hall, and Carolyn Lloyd-Brown. *Viking Ships.* Information pack for Viking Ships exhibition at St. Saviour's Archaeological Resource Centre, St. Saviourgate, York, England, 1987.

Vikings! Traders and Craftsmen. Exhibition catalog. Seattle: Nordic Heritage Museum, 1984.

The Vikings Exhibition. Ottawa: National Gallery of Canada, 1968.

INDEX

TIME® LIFE BOOKS

Time-Life Books is a division of Time Life Inc.

TIME LIFE INC.
PRESIDENT and CEO: George Artandi

TIME-LIFE BOOKS
PRESIDENT: Stephen R. Frary
PUBLISHER/MANAGING EDITOR: Neil Kagan

What Life Was Like ®
WHEN LONGSHIPS SAILED

EDITOR: Denise Dersin
DIRECTOR, NEW PRODUCT DEVELOPMENT:
Elizabeth D. Ward
DIRECTORS OF MARKETING:
Pamela R. Farrell, Joseph A. Kuna

Deputy Editor: Marion Ferguson Briggs
Art Director: Alan Pitts
Text Editor: Stephen G. Hyslop
Associate Editors/Research and Writing:
Jarelle S. Stein, Sharon Kurtz Thompson
Senior Copyeditor: Mary Beth Oelkers-Keegan
Technical Art Specialist: John Drummond
Picture Coordinator: David Herod
Editorial Assistant: Christine Higgins

Special Contributors: Charlotte Anker, Dónal Kevin Gordon, Ellen Phillips (chapter text); Gaye Brown, Christine Hauser, Elizabeth Thompson, Myrna Traylor-Herndon (research-writing); Arlene Borden, Jessica K. Ferrell, Beth Levin (research); James Michael Lynch (editing); Lina Baber Burton (glossary); Barbara L. Klein (index and overread).

Correspondents: Maria Vincenza Aloisi (Paris), Christine Hinze (London), Christina Lieberman (New York). Valuable assistance was also provided by: Dag Christensen (Oslo), Barbara Gevene Hertz (Copenhagen), Andrew Keith (Moscow), Angelika Lemmer (Bonn).

Director of Finance: Christopher Hearing
Directors of Book Production: Marjann Caldwell, Patricia Pascale
Director of Publishing Technology: Betsi McGrath
Director of Photography and Research: John Conrad Weiser
Director of Editorial Administration: Barbara Levitt
Production Manager: Gertraude Schaefer
Quality Assurance Manager: James King
Chief Librarian: Louise D. Forstall

Consultant:
Richard N. Ringler received his Ph.D. from Harvard University and is currently professor of English and Scandinavian Studies at the University of Wisconsin-Madison, specializing in the history, language, and literature of Anglo-Saxon England and Medieval Scandinavia. He has published numerous books and articles in both fields. Dr. Ringler also studied at the University of Iceland in Reykjavik and traveled to the Orkneys, Shetlands, and Hebrides to study the early Viking westward expansion. He is an expert on the language and literature of modern Iceland.

First printing. Printed in U.S.A.
Published simultaneously in Canada.
School and library distribution by Time-Life Education, P.O. Box 85026, Richmond, Virginia 23285-5026.

TIME-LIFE is a trademark of Time Warner Inc. U.S.A.

Library of Congress Cataloging-in-Publication Data
What life was like when longships sailed : Vikings
AD 800-1100 / by the editors of Time-Life Books.
    p. cm.
    Includes bibliographical references and index.
    ISBN 0-7835-5454-0
    1. Vikings. 2. Europe—History—476-1492.
I. Time-Life Books.
DL65.W53 1998   97-40845
948'—dc21   CIP

Other Publications:
HISTORY
The American Story
Voices of the Civil War
The American Indians
Lost Civilizations
Mysteries of the Unknown
Time Frame
The Civil War
Cultural Atlas

COOKING
Weight Watchers® Smart Choice Recipe Collection
Great Taste~Low Fat
Williams-Sonoma Kitchen Library

SCIENCE/NATURE
Voyage Through the Universe

DO IT YOURSELF
The Time-Life Complete Gardener
Home Repair and Improvement
The Art of Woodworking
Fix It Yourself

TIME-LIFE KIDS
Library of First Questions and Answers
A Child's First Library of Learning
I Love Math
Nature Company Discoveries
Understanding Science & Nature

For information on and a full description of any of the Time-Life Books series listed above, please call 1-800-621-7026 or write:

Reader Information
Time-Life Customer Service
P.O. Box C-32068
Richmond, Virginia 23261-2068

This volume is one in a series on world history that uses contemporary art, artifacts, and personal accounts to create an intimate portrait of daily life in the past.

Other volumes included in the
What Life Was Like series:

On the Banks of the Nile: Egypt, 3050-30 BC
In the Age of Chivalry: Medieval Europe, AD 800-1500
When Rome Ruled the World: The Roman Empire, 100 BC-AD 200
At the Dawn of Democracy: Classical Athens, 525-322 BC
Among Druids and High Kings: Celtic Ireland, AD 400-1200